FIFTY YEARS
CONFIDENCE

SIMON GILL and **KEN WILLIAMS**

'The feeling or belief that one can have faith in or rely on someone or something'

Definition of 'Confidence' by the lexicographers at Oxford Dictionaries

Fifty Years of Confidence

First Published in 2020 by
Simon Gill Publishing
1A Penkridge Bank Road,
Rugeley, Staffordshire, WS15 2UE

ISBN 978-1-5272-5730-6

Copyright © Simon Gill 2020

Design and layout by Russell Strong

Printed by Lavenham Press
www.lavenhampress.co.uk

Front cover photographs:
Top: **One of many Olympians, No 57 (A139 SMA).**
Bottom, left to right: **Nos 89 (T325 LAF),
22 (OTO 570M), 36 (VRC 611Y) and 15 (WLT 655).**

Rear cover photographs
Top: **No 5 as Southdown 1749 (749 DCD).**
Centre, left: **No 1 as Southdown 547 (PUF 647).**
Centre, right: **No 34 as Barton 564 (KAU 564V).**
Bottom: **The new Volvo B9TL, No 71 (FJ58 CON).**
All: Simon Gill

Contents

Title page: **The longest serving bus in the Confidence fleet is No 15 (WLT 655) an AEC Routemaster with Park Royal body new to London Transport in 1961. It has been owned since 1985 and is seen awaiting departure for the 'RM50 Anniversary' at Finsbury Park on 24 July 2004.** Simon Gill

Foreword

The idea for this book originated ten years ago with the intention of celebrating the 40th Anniversary of Confidence. Lack of time to produce it during 2010 resulted in the project being deferred.

After taking early retirement from a busy career in the finance industry I was asked to contribute articles to 'Bus & Coach Preservation' magazine and the enjoyment derived from writing these gave me the added impetus to get this book done, to coin a well used phrase from the past few months.

My interest in Confidence began as a teenager when, looking out of my bedroom window, I first saw a grey and black double deck bus parked on the main car park in Oadby, Leicestershire. Closer inspection revealed it was Confidence No 1, the Guy Arab and I remember being delighted to see a new independent operator in the county using a double deck bus when so many were disappearing from the area.

The arrival of interesting coaches and another double-decker added to my enthusiasm but, suddenly, they all vanished to the other side of the county. What a disappointment. I still got the occasional sight of one in Oadby or Leicester going about their business of providing school transport but, unfortunately, not at my school.

Later, after getting married and moving house to just around the corner from Ken Williams, I got to know him and a friendship was formed that has continued ever since. Membership of the Leicester area of the Birmingham & Midland Motor Omnibus Trust (now the Transport Museum, Wythall) and the Leicester Transport Heritage Trust (and its forerunners) enabled me to develop friendships with other local enthusiasts, many of whom are acknowledged on page four. Their help and encouragement is gratefully appreciated.

The book is split into two parts. In the first section, Ken shares some of his early memories, describes how Confidence came about and some of the decisions that has enabled the business to be where it is today. My contribution has been researching the history of the fleet and piecing it all together. I am grateful to Ken for all his help and enthusiasm.

We hope you enjoy it. Simon Gill, March 2020

No 5 (749 DCD) the Leyland Leopard with Harrington Grenadier body parked on Oadby car park where I saw my first Confidence bus. My parent's house was on the opposite side of the road on the left immediately behind it. Simon Gill

Introduction

Not just the school bus – the CONFIDENCE school bus!

Confidence is a small privately owned Bus and Coach Company in Leicester which started in May 1970, is still going strong, and very proud to be celebrating its 50th Anniversary in 2020.

Operations are mostly aimed at the schools market and not many people under the age of 55 who went to school in Leicester have not ridden on a Confidence bus, whether they wanted to or not. The fleet name and livery were inspired by an early career in the Merchant Navy on a tanker named 'British Confidence'.

Many people think the buses they rode on are the same ones that are around now – sometimes they are as many have been operated for longer than their original or previous owner kept them – but the fleet has been updated over the years. Maybe you went to school, or to the swimming baths, on a Confidence bus? If so, which generation of the fleet did you travel on?

It may be surprising to some that only 90 vehicles have been operated so far, of which only one has been bought new.

Confidence has always operated to the following important values and principles:

1. If we can't afford it, we can't have it
2. Only borrow money to buy property, not vehicles, and then only affordable property
3. Don't overreach and don't promise anything you can't do (A 20 year old double deck bus is not, and never will be, an all singing, all dancing luxury coach so don't try and kid anybody)
4. Remember, the tax you pay on this year's income is paid next year – Don't spend it!

Yes, they are cautious but that's the Confidence way.

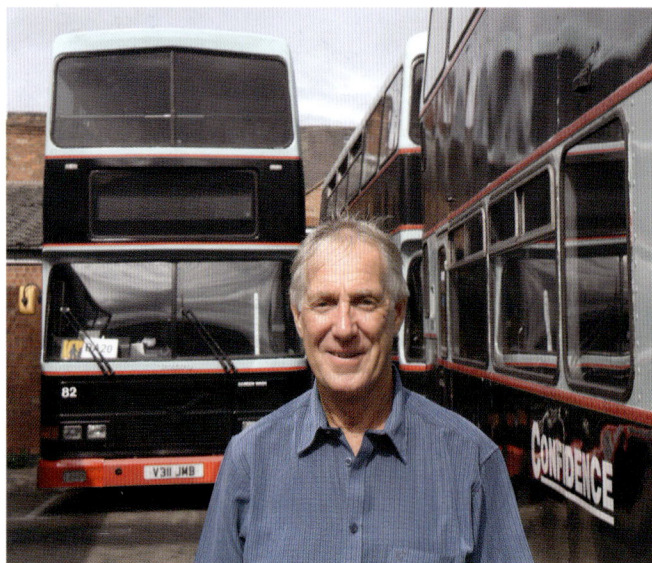

We would not have achieved fifty years serving the people and school children of Leicester and Leicestershire without the support of our employees, suppliers, family, friends, dealers and everyone who has helped us during this period. I have chosen not to name anyone as I would be upset if I missed anybody. To you all, a heartfelt, THANK YOU!

Whilst I prefer not to name individual employees, anyone contacting Confidence since the autumn of 1988 will, most probably, have spoken to Malveena. She has been an instrumental part of Confidence's success and continues to be so.

Finally, I would like to thank Simon Gill for his idea to do this book. Without his drive and enthusiasm it would not have been possible.

Ken Williams, March 2020

Acknowledgements

The authors are grateful to a number of individuals and organisations who have helped to make this 50th Anniversary book possible. In particular, The PSV Circle kindly agreed to allow us to use information from their news sheets and publications, Fred Ward provided additional detail and Dick White allowed us access to his records. Gerry Tormey provided details of the Leyland Olympians built in Bristol. The history of BP Tankers was provided by Bob Fleming and Richard Worman kindly contributed his driving record.

We are also indebted to a number of websites that provide details of vehicles including: Bus Lists on the Web, Ian's Bus Stop and Classic Irish Buses.

A number of photographers have kindly allowed us to use images they have taken, or are available from their collections, often at short notice. They are gratefully acknowledged after the caption to each photograph but we would especially like to thank Adrian Rodgers for access to his extensive collection, Trevor Follows, Mike Greenwood, Steve Smith, Tom Moore, Chris Aston of Omnicolour, Peter Cordwell, Peter Newland, Colin Billington, Ray Bignall, Ian Manning, Eric Wain and Andrew Tucker.

Finally, special thanks to my wife Jan for proofreading the text and allowing me the time to research and write this book, Paul Gill for producing the graphs and Russell Strong for his design skills.

Left: **Ken Williams.** Simon Gill

Opposite page: **The second longest serving bus in the fleet is No 46 (UWW 8X), a Leyland Olympian with Roe body that was new to West Yorkshire PTE in March 1982. It is seen in Leicester City Centre about to depart on an excursion on 19 May 2019.** Simon Gill

Chapter 1

The Child

The first word I could say was 'mom' – probably in a Birmingham accent as that was where I was born. The second word was 'buzz'… most definitely in the Birmingham style!

Birmingham City Transport route 28 (City – Kingstanding – Great Barr) passed the door of our house. One day during 1945 – 1949 I was found at the crossroads of Hawthorne Road and College Road as a toddler. What did I see that day? Midland Red SONs, DONs, FEDDS, wartime Guys and Daimlers. Wow! I can't remember now but it was wonderful.

The family then moved to Shirley, south of Birmingham. We lived in Colebrook Croft and at the Colebrook Road corner there was a grass bank with a small concrete post which made a super spot to sit and watch buses. The low bridge to the left carried the Stratford-upon-Avon to Birmingham railway line and under the bridge travelled the 170/172 Midland Red bus routes between Acocks Green and Wythall. It must have been mostly BMMO S8s and S9s on these services due to the low bridge, with GWR Prairie Tanks pulling the trains above, although we also got big engines and a diesel railcar which was a special treat.

At school, a converted church on Stratford Road, Shirley, it was all Midland Red. I would occasionally spot a blue and cream

Stratford Blue bus and also sometimes see a Birmingham bus with the coat of arms painted out, going away from Birmingham, probably on its final journey to Bird's scrap yard at Stratford-upon-Avon. Again, it was wonderful.

To get into town it was a walk down Acheson Road to the Art Deco-style Baldwin Public House to catch a Birmingham City Transport 29A bus which ran across the city to Kingstanding where my grandmother lived. It was operated mostly by brand new Birmingham Standards. How I loved those buses.

Highlights of the 29A journey to town included passing Smith's Imperial Coaches, the tram tracks joining the route in the Bordesley area (I never saw a tram there) and the Bird's Custard factory. I still love custard. We did see and ride on Birmingham trams to Aston and also passed what many people called bomb sites. I didn't realise at the time that they were actual bomb sites where people had been killed and made homeless many years previously. To a young lad they just seemed part of the scenery.

My memories include getting off the 29A at the Bull Ring and seeing an old lady (she seemed old to me) selling handy strong brown paper carrier bags to the passengers as they got off. Another memory was going up the steps to the roofless marketplace to see the bomb that presumably went through the roof and failed to explode. I also remember going to Lewis's department store to see Santa. I spotted him from the top deck of the bus on Stratford Road and he got to Lewis's before us. I didn't believe in Santa after that, but still loved going to Lewis's to see him for the present.

If my dad was feeling flush we would go on the train. I always remember the enjoyment of watching the locomotive disconnect from the carriages and go on to the traverser at the buffers at Moor Street Station to move over to the adjoining track so it could run round the train.

My dad told me I couldn't have my own bus company. He said I could work on the buses but all the buses in Birmingham were owned by the Corporation or Midland Red. I couldn't have my own railway train either, I thought, because I haven't got any track.

Trains and buses…what was their appeal to this scruffy kid?

Other than the bus ride, I can't say visiting my gran was much fun; 'little boys should be seen and not heard' was her greeting, but I loved the journey. Now I was 8 years old and more grown up, my mom used to put me and Brian, my younger brother, on the bus at The Baldwin with instructions to the conductor to put us off at

Birmingham City Transport 3225 (MOF 225) is a Daimler CVG6 with Crossley 55-seat bodywork new in October 1954. It is now preserved in the heritage fleet of National Express West Midlands. It was photographed in Lichfield on 1 September 2018. Simon Gill

A unique bus, sometimes used on the 29A route, was Birmingham City Transport 3002 (LOG 302), a lightweight Daimler CLG5 with Metro-Cammell 55-seat body new in October 1954. It is now preserved and is seen at the Aston Manor Road Transport Museum, Aldridge on 28 April 2019. Simon Gill

One of the first Birmingham 'Standards' that impressed Ken was 2548 (JOJ 548), a Guy Arab with Metro-Cammell 54-seat body new in October 1950. Now preserved, it attended the Buses Festival at Gaydon on 18 August 2019. Simon Gill

Kingstanding where my gran would meet us. I don't think she ever did, but not to worry, we knew the route and the way. Incredibly, a book was written about the 29A in 2013 which was very informative – 'Across Birmingham on the 29A' by David Harvey.

Brian and I would sit at the front of the top deck. The kid that sat on the other front seat – was he the author I wonder?

I would observe every bus and coach we saw. Those Birmingham Corporation buses were gorgeous, hundreds of them all looking the same until you studied them, and then they weren't. That one's a Guy, that one's a Crossley, oh a Leyland, an AEC and what's that – a Daimler? Then there was Midland Red. What is this wonderful world I had been born into? Hundreds of buses, no thousands, all owned by corporations; Birmingham, West Bromwich, Walsall or the mighty Midland Red. Even the occasional Stratford Blue bus was owned by Midland Red. I thought my dad said you couldn't have your own bus company…

Our new school opened at Burman Road which was nearer to home and off the beaten track. The only memories I have are builders of houses near the school singing 'Jezebel' (a successful single by Frankie Laine released in 1951) and one day we were all sent to the hall to be informed that the King had died. What! I didn't know a King could die – I thought Kings were exempt.

MANDY RICE-DAVIES (21 October 1944 - 18 December 2014)

Born Marilyn Davies, she was a model, dancer and showgirl who achieved fame for her association with Christine Keeler and her role in the Profumo Affair which discredited the Conservative government of Harold Macmillan in 1963. Although born in Wales she moved to Solihull as a child, with her family. She went on to become a successful actress and businesswoman.

The next school I attended was Haslucks Green Junior School, just off Stratford Road. Memories include collecting cigarette cards of buses – we all wanted the Birmingham one – and weaving. I had nightmares about weaving. Why were we learning weaving? We lived in Birmingham! I also remember a new kid who came from Hong Kong. He taught me to say 'yap', 'he', 'son', 'say' – 1, 2, 3, 4. However, when I was lucky enough to visit Hong Kong many years later, I tried the words out and just got vacant looks.

Also, was Mandy Rice-Davies in my class?

Another Guy Arab with Metro-Cammell 55-seat body preserved is 3009 (MOF 9) new in July 1953. Birmingham Standards had straight stairs rather than the right angle turn half way up that most operators used. Simon Gill

Chapter 2

The Boy

In 1953, aged 8¾, my parents moved to Leicester. A bit different to Birmingham – for a start we had sunshine. I hadn't seen much of that in industrial Birmingham after the war. What interested me though were the different buses; more names, more colours but still the mighty Midland Red.

What was it about Midland Red? I loved them. I would find out in time but now, at St Margaret's Bus Station in Leicester, where we caught our Midland Red bus L29 to Scraptoft Lane, there were other buses. Red and cream, red and maroon, blue and red, blue and cream, maroon and cream. These buses weren't owned by Leicester Corporation – they had their own fleet, and not by Midland Red. So could you own your own bus company?

I soon settled in Leicester with new school friends and got the nickname 'big brummie', my brother, 'little brummie' because we spoke funny. We had to go to school by bus. Wow! Guess who – Midland Red. My new found friends and I had many debates about buses. They, defending their love of Leicester's maroon and cream which I always said was brown, with me extolling the virtues of Birmingham buses. I have still got the bruises.

I think my enthusiasm for buses rubbed off on all my new friends, Ray, Vic, Spill and Gordon. We all discovered that railway engines also had numbers like buses.

Gordon's dad was able to get fleet lists of all the Midland Red buses and he gave us one each. Bus spotting then really took off. I had the advantage of a gran, grandad, uncle and auntie still in Birmingham so frequent trips on the magic X68 Leicester - Coventry

- Birmingham on a new BMMO D7 or sometimes an LD8, meant I collected far more numbers than the others. Also, again, if my dad could afford it we travelled by train, usually a Stanier or Fowler tank engine. There was so much to learn, so much to take in.

One of my current pleasures is to go on a day out with old and new friends, including Ray, Vic and Spill and we still talk and reminisce about trains and buses. Sadly Gordon died some years ago.

I know bus or train spotting is regarded as being 'nerdy' but our knowledge of geography or other events became brilliant. When Midland Red bus number 3093 was known to be at Wellington Depot and you hadn't seen it, out came the maps to discover where it could be found.

Nowadays young kids are not in to such things as most only travel by car. I rather think that, unless things change, there are not going to be many bus and train enthusiasts in the future as they are not going to come into contact with them, which is so sad.

Junior school at Thurnby was good – the journey to and from wonderful! Two Midland Reds came to Thurnby; the one from Stoughton always seemingly using the oldest pre-war single deck bus they could find. Ours from Scraptoft Lane had the delights of S6s, S9s, S10s and the then new S13s. One of the S9s, No 3441 (LHA 441) was special with power doors and American style aluminium trim fitted by Carlyle Works before entering service. It was always a Leicester Sandiacre garage bus. We had one conductor who some of the older boys could easily wind up and

Left: **Awaiting departure from St Margaret's bus station on the L29 to Scraptoft Green is Midland Red 4893 (893 KHA) a BMMO D9 with Carlyle 72-seat body new in 1960. On the right about to head for Loughborough on the 625 is 4552 (XHA 552) a BMMO D7 with Metro-Cammell 63-seat body new in 1957.** Mike Greenwood Collection

Opposite, top: **One of the buses Ken may have travelled on was Midland Red LD8 no 4013 (SHA 413), a 1953 Leyland Titan PD2/12 with Leyland 56-seat body and 'new look' BMMO enclosed front grille. It awaits departure on the X68 to Birmingham at Southgate Street bus station, Leicester.** Omnicolour

Opposite, bottom: **Friends for over 60 years (from left to right) Steve Hill (Spill), Ray Bishop, me, Vic Chawner enjoying a trip to Euston Station, London on LMS Princess Coronation Class 6233, Duchess of Sutherland.** Ken Williams Collection

he went bright red in the face (nearly the same colour as the bus) when shouting at us.

The school dentist was the fly in the ointment. Working through the register in alphabetical order and with my surname being Williams, I was one of the last to be seen. So all week I watched my classmates coming back in agony knowing it would be Friday afternoon, when he was tired, before I would be seen. No injections, no gas and a clamp in the mouth while be peddled his drill – no electric drills in those days. We all had fillings but why did we need them when sugar was on ration and we didn't eat sweets? I hated the school dentist and think he must have been on commission.

Next, Brian and I went to Oadby Gartree Modern School as it was known then; it is now called Gartree High School. Travel this time was by local coach operator Cleavers using Bedford SBs, Commer Avengers and an unusual Dennis. I can still hear the Commer's engine ringing in my ears. If you had told me, as an 11-year-old, that one day I would operate this very same journey with my own buses I would not have believed it; after all, you can't have your own bus company can you?

My next school was Guthlaxton Grammar School in Wigston. This time travel was courtesy of Northend Motors with our coach, a half-cab Dennis, coming from Toones of Billesdon who Northend had, at that time, recently acquired.

School was okay but there was more to life so I did two morning paper rounds and one afternoon paper round for Mr Facer, plus grocery deliveries for Mr Hextall, both of Parkstone Road, which

produced some pocket money. Together with a few friends we also used to go 'gateing' where we opened and closed the cattle gates on the lane from Scraptoft to Hamilton for the occasional motorist, often getting a tip, until the farmer caught us when we closed the gate he had left open.

The money came in useful as Midland Red had introduced a Day Anywhere ticket that cost five shillings. You bought your ticket in advance and the date of travel was stamped on it. Gosh, this was like a passport. Midland Red route maps came out and were

Freshly repainted Midland Red 3704 (NHA 704) is a 1950 BMMO S10 with Metro-Cammell body passing Stoughton Church in April 1966. Omnicolour

Ken remembers this unique Midland Red S9 Mk 1 very well due to its American style trim. No 3441 (LHA 441) was new in 1949 with a Brush body that was rebuilt at Carlyle works. It is seen at St Margaret's bus station, Leicester in August 1963. Omnicolour

Another type that Ken was keen to spot was Midland Red 3744 (NHA 744). One of the first deliveries built to the increased length of 30ft it is a BMMO S12 with Brush 44-seat body new in 1950. It is now preserved at the Transport Museum, Wythall. Simon Gill

spread all over the floor to plan the day out. Most times a friend came along but sometimes I would travel on my own. The object was to travel to towns and cities with a bus garage. There were 33 of them and I went to them all. As the days ticked by until the date of travel, excitement mounted until the night before, when going to sleep was extremely difficult.

The map showed Leicester as the north east outpost with three garages but the buses did venture much further north and east, such as Grantham where we usually travelled on a BMMO D7 to begin our train spotting expeditions, but I am digressing. The south east extreme was Banbury and the most south westerly town with a garage was Hereford, but my favourite was the north west extremity, Shrewsbury. Even to this day I still look out for Shrewsbury Town FC's football results.

Just look at a map and envisage us kids, or me on my own, going off on a jaunt. No mobile phones then – even our houses didn't have landlines. In any event I didn't know when to press button A or button B, never mind having four pennies to spare.

I never ever got stuck and never had a bus break down or not turn up. Most inter town routes where operated by double-deckers with the BMMO D7 the most likely type – I loved them. Imagine my dad when I came home at about 10:30pm, on a Saturday, aged 14. He would ask me where I'd been and I would say Birmingham, Kidderminster, Ludlow, Hereford and Worcester – all for five shillings. I had a notebook full of bus numbers which included very few that you would see in Leicester.

We had some good school teachers. We were able to get them to arrange trips to Crewe railway works but, best of all, we had a trip to Edgbaston, Birmingham. Carlyle Works was where Midland Red built their own buses. This was Britain in the 1950s and not only did they build them, they designed them there as well – they were so advanced. In 1954 they introduced the S14, a single deck bus that, remarkably, only weighed just over 5 tons and, with 44 seats, it did around 18 miles per gallon. Try to buy a 44-seat single deck bus nowadays and you can't. Perhaps 38 or 39 seats is the maximum and it will weigh 11 tons and do four miles per gallon.

Our trip to the works was great. They used to build 2 to 3 buses per week so on the production lines we saw S14s/S15s and D9s. Some would still be many weeks away from entering service. Their numbers were quickly noted in the book and that was the best I ever got. Out of 1,856 Midland Red buses there were only six that I never saw. One, No 3000 (HHA 601), was the first BMMO S6. Based at Bromsgrove I made several visits to the town but still never saw it.

I earned more money when I was at school than when I started work. I got a Friday night and Saturday job at a new sensation; a giant grocery store called Tesco. This was in Lee Circle, Leicester with a multi-storey car park above. It was the first Tesco outside London and claimed to be the biggest supermarket in Britain at the time it opened in 1960. I still had Sundays free and it was a good job bus services were good in those days so I could continue to go on my jaunts.

I was in the store once when the manager had a panic. Mr and Mrs Cohen, the proprietors of Tesco, were making a fleeting visit to their premier supermarket. The manager told me 'make sure you stand at the door and give everybody a basket'. That was easier

OBC 702 was a Commer Avenger Mk III with a Duple 41-seat body new in December 1955 to Harry Cleaver (Leicester) Ltd of Green Lane Road, Leicester. It was given fleet number 19 and passed to Barkus, Woodhouse Eaves in May 1961. Leicester Transport Heritage Trust Archive

Cleavers No 36 (XRY 270) was a Commer Avenger Mk IV with Duple Corinthian 41-seat body new in March 1960. It passed to Ashman, Leicester in January 1964. The late Derek Bailey/Trevor Follows Collection

Ken's favourite double deck bus was the BMMO D7 with Metro-Cammell 63-seat body. Midland Red 4482 (XHA 482), built in 1956 stands next to BMMO S14, 4255 (UHA 255) built the previous year. They are both preserved at the Transport Museum, Wythall. Simon Gill

said than done. Remember, this was the first supermarket. Burley blokes did not want to walk around with a pansy basket and told me so in no uncertain terms. I was 14 years old and weighed about eight stone and wanted to make age 15 and maybe eight stone and a bit. Anyway most blokes didn't have a basket. Mr Cohen and his wife came in. He was not much bigger than me which put me at ease.

'Why are you standing there?' he bellowed, 'most people look to the left when they walk, you are standing on the right'. Oh god, I had been told off by Mr Tesco. Later, the manager came and found me. 'Take Mr and Mrs Cohen's groceries to the car' (What? They hadn't come by bus!). That I duly did and Mrs Cohen gave me sixpence as a tip which was quite a bit then; I've never forgotten that.

Suddenly, school was over and it was time to venture into the big wide world.

Chapter 3

The Apprentice

I obtained a five year craft apprenticeship at a Leicester engineering firm called Jones and Shipman. I earned less than before but was assured it would be a job for life.

I'm not sure I wanted a job for life – what about the buses? Anyway it would be good training and I would learn a skill.

My best friends Ray, Vic and Spill all got similar jobs and Gordon ended up training in agriculture. He always did have a strange fascination for rabbits.

To avoid mickey taking I decided to pack up bus and train spotting but still kept an eye on both industries, occasionally enjoying the delights of Midland Red Day Anywhere tickets. The winter of 1962/63 was the coldest in years. Engineers and transport workers in the rail and bus industries were heroes and I gave up riding my bike for several months. I also gave up playing football. The final decision was made when riding my bicycle to an away game in freezing conditions, changing rooms frozen solid, the pitch like concrete and riding home crying with hot aches, thinking I didn't enjoy that. I could have stayed at home jockeying for position with my brother to sit in front of the one bar electric fire – he had had it all to himself. So ended any future career I might have had as a football star.

My apprenticeship went okay only to be interrupted by a holiday accident with Ray. We had booked a summer holiday in 1963 to Skegness. It was our first holiday staying in a hotel without our parents. We had enjoyed previous cycling holidays, youth

The main bus operator in Skegness was Lincolnshire Road Car Company which ran a number of Bristol Lodekkas with Eastern Coach Works (ECW) bodies. No 2318 (LFW 326) was a LD6B model with 58-seat body new in April 1955. It is now preserved by the Lincolnshire Vintage Vehicle Society. Simon Gill

The flat terrain of Lincolnshire suited the low powered Bristol SC4LK. Lincolnshire 2494 (RFE 482) with ECW 35-seat body was new in August 1961 and is now part of the Stagecoach Yorkshire heritage fleet. Simon Gill

hostelling with friends to Norfolk and once to Devon and Cornwall, but those were different.

We were on the big wheel going round when, near the bottom, we heard a loud crack. My side of the chair dropped down and Ray slid along the seat squeezing up against me. Because the chair's axle on my side had become dislodged it remained in the fixed position which prevented the chair from swiveling. As we went higher the chair remained fixed to the wheel so, instead of staying upright in the sitting position, we ended up dangling upside down with only the handrail under our stomachs for support, whilst looking down through the wheel, daring not to move. The wheel was still going round.

We then heard another cracking noise and I fainted – sorry, I was no James Bond! The next I knew, I was on the ground trying to get up and walk away but I couldn't. Ray was lying nearby. We had both fallen through the wheel, missing girders, framework, other seats and a perimeter fence on to concrete.

Ray and I shared an ambulance with a girl injured by our chair falling through the wheel and another lady suffering from shock who passed out whilst watching from the ground. The next day the headline of our local newspaper, the *Leicester Mercury*, pronounced 'Teenagers plunge 30 feet from Big Wheel'. It was our claim to fame.

The fall left me with a badly damaged left elbow (is that why I struggled to drive a manual Leyland Tiger?), facial injuries and

the loss of a couple of teeth. Some would say I also incurred brain damage as I still dreamt of buying a bus.

I had my left elbow pinned which proved to be very successful. Only on one occasion did it give me any trouble and I had an operation to remove the pin. Unfortunately, it sheared off so half the pin is still with me – rather like me fixing a bus. My left arm is not as flexible as normal and my left hand is smaller than my right hand. That said, I think I stopped growing at 17 years old so it's a good job I didn't fall off the wheel when I was 10. Incredibly, three months later I was back at work so had been very lucky.

Ray was much worse. He didn't faint but broke both arms in several places and shattered his knee cap in an attempt to break his fall. He took a year to recover. We were not meant to die yet – there were still plenty more bus rides to enjoy.

The remainder of my apprenticeship continued uneventfully, although I was not enjoying it and did apply for a couple of other jobs before my time was up. My dad told me to stick at it because at 21 years of age I would have a skill to fall back on. He was right. A couple of months before my 21st birthday I applied for, and got, a position as a Junior Engineer on BP tankers – not the road ones, but the marine ones. My life was about to change dramatically.

Chapter 4

The Officer

After visits to Birmingham for medical checks and injections – how on earth did I get home after that typhoid jab? – I then had to travel to London to get my officer's uniform – yes, believe it or not I was an officer, albeit a junior one.

It was not long before I received a telegram. It is hard to imagine telegrams in this day and age but it was, after all, 1966, steam trains were still running and we still had no telephone in our house. Times were still tough and if you received an apple and an orange for Christmas that's all you got – not an iPad or mobile phone which some people are lucky enough to receive now. The telegram said 'Report to Cowes Road, Southampton at such and such a time. Travel Warrant will follow', which it duly did.

Nervously, I wore my new uniform and set off for Southampton by train at the appointed time. On arrival I had to find an office in the city centre and was told to wait. I did see some Guy Arabs belonging to Southampton City Transport whist I was waiting, which was comforting. After a while I was taken to the quayside and got onto a small boat which eventually set off down the Solent. We seemed to be sailing for ages with the Isle of Wight on the right and Portsmouth on the left until, moored in the middle of the water loomed this giant ship. I thought, wow it's huge, the biggest ship I had ever seen. This was to be my new home.

As the small boat drew up close I saw, dangling over the side of the ship, a rope ladder which must have been 40 feet from water level to the ship's deck. Next to it was a rope with a hook for my suitcase and before I knew it the suitcase had gone – hauled aboard the ship. I started to panic a little; surely I've not got to climb up the rope ladder? Did I mention falling off the Big Wheel to Mr BP? Ah well, if I fall I suppose water is softer than concrete so off I went, tentatively climbing up and finally clambering over the railings. Wow, the ship was massive. I didn't know anything about it as we didn't get them in Leicester and I had not seen any at Skegness or Blackpool!

The ship was named 'British Commerce'. A 65,000 ton oil tanker, its purpose was to collect crude oil and deliver it to oil terminals for refining into products such as fuel oils (petrol/diesel), plastics, fine oils etc. I was shown to my cabin via a peep into the engine room. I stood at the top of the engine room and looked down. Oh my god, a giant nine cylinder in-line diesel engine was the main feature, but it was like a factory with pipes, gangways, steps, platforms and machines all in a maze. I was in a daze as I continued to my cabin where I was told to settle in and then report to the Second Engineer for my duties. All the crew knew I was new due to my uniform – I never joined a ship in uniform again!

It was with shock that I learnt there were only eight engineers and one electrician aboard the ship, together with a similar number of navigating officers, about 10 crew members and five or six caterers to sail this huge vessel 24-hours a day, seven days a week.

My word it was hard work but it made me. In contrast, Jones and Shipman was a great firm but I had coasted during my time there.

The ship depended on the engineers and electrician to survive and I was one of them. It was a major learning curve.

I was soon in the engine room, so much to learn, so much to absorb and oh, so noisy. As well as the engine having nine cylinders in a straight line each piston was one metre in diameter, banging up and down at about 105 revs per minute. The engine was about 45 feet long (nearly the length of two 1950s buses), 15 feet from top to bottom, 6 feet wide at the top and about 15 feet wide at the bottom. It was awesome – was this the biggest diesel engine ever?

To start the engine compressed air was used to turn it, blown into the cylinder heads until it picked up and drove itself. Each cylinder had its own fuel injection pump and it ran on heavy oil. I was later to learn that it was troublesome as well.

It was not just the engine, the ship was like a small town needing electricity, water and steam all generated in the engine room. We had boilers to produce steam which was used to heat the cargo as crude oil becomes solid in the cold – the oil tanks were lined with steam pipes to prevent this happening. Steam was also used to power deck machinery as there was no electric on deck in case of sparks. Electricity was used for lighting, cooking and heating with fresh water for washing, drinking and cooking. Diesel generators produced the electricity with condensers used for boiling seawater, catching the steam and condensing it into distilled water – you got used to drinking it. All this kit plus bilge pumps to pump out waste and the biggest prop shaft you have ever seen. It all had to be kept going, maintained and logged. We carried lots of spare parts, including a spare piston assembly, and even had a small workshop for use when required.

The working pattern saw one of the three Senior Engineers, usually a Fourth Engineer or one of two Third Engineers taking a watch each, accompanied by a Junior Engineer. A watch was four hours on and eight hours off so, in theory, if you were on 4 to 8 shift you did 4 o'clock until 8 o'clock, AM and PM then the next watch did 8 to 12 and the final one 12 until 4. The Second Engineer and Electrician did days and the Chief Engineer, wisely, kept out of the way. Maybe there was one apprentice but otherwise that was the total engineering staff.

It soon came to light that four hours on and eight hours off was a misnomer. When the ship had problems the emergency alarm went off and we all had to report 'on the plates' to use engine room terminology. Also, sailing east to west or vice versa involved constantly 'flogging the clocks'; adjusting the time so it got light in the morning and dark at night and ensured when we arrived at a destination we had the same time as them. If we broke down at sea – and we did – we couldn't call the AA. It was us – we were the AA.

So off we went heading to the Persian Gulf via the Mediterranean Sea and Suez Canal which was very exciting. We then loaded up in the Gulf and went to Sardinia, then back to Libya and back to Sardinia again before going back through the Suez Canal towards the Gulf. We had just entered the Red Sea when war broke out in Egypt and the Suez closed. Many ships were marooned in the Suez Canal or the halfway passing point, the Bitter Lakes, for months or even years. Luckily, we got through only to experience engine trouble.

That spare piston was needed and we had to fit it so we were drifting around in the Red Sea whilst we 'Pulled the piston' and had to fit the new one. Although I was bigger than when I was at Tesco's I was still no heavyweight and those cylinder head nuts were huge. To undo it there was a spanner I could hardly pick up and a sledgehammer to hit it with. It was a good job the electrician was a big lad – we all worked all day in addition to doing our usual watches.

We had an overhead gantry to carry the heavy parts and lift the piston. We had just got the piston in the air hanging from the gantry when the ship started to roll. A storm brewed up and we had this massive piston swinging about in the engine room. It was time to get out of the way. The storm subsided and amazingly we fitted the new piston and got underway again.

One of the Guy Arab III's that Ken saw whilst he was waiting for the boat could have been Southampton City Transport 71 (LOW 217). Fitted with a Park Royal 56-seat body in 1954 it has been preserved and is now looked after by the Southampton & District Transport Heritage Trust. Doesn't it look old compared to the year older Midland Red LD8 on page 9? Simon Gill

Whilst drifting some of the crew members, deckhands and caterers put a lump of meat on a hook, tied to a rope and dangled it over the poop (back end) of the ship. Sure enough, a shark bit the meat and got hooked. A group of men started to haul the rope onto the deck with me watching from a safe distance. The shark was angry, flapping and tossing whilst the men pulled it up the side of the ship. It got up to the railings violently trying to get free and I worried that if it got on deck it would get somebody. Its mouth ripped open and it fell back into the sea with blood streaming from it. The next moment other sharks came and attacked it and it was gone. I will never forget that moment or the time flying fish landed on deck and promptly sizzled because the steel decks were red hot.

Back in the engine room the fuel pipes to the engine used to vibrate and the couplings tended to shear. This often resulted in thick heavy oil squirting all over the place at high pressure. We were running out of couplings but, thanks to my days at Jones and Shipman, I was the only one who could use a lathe, so I was put on days for a while to manufacture a new supply. I was quite proud of my couplings as they lasted much longer than the originals.

After this point all trips to the Persian Gulf from Europe had to travel all around Africa. This resulted in BP withdrawing some of the smaller ships as they consumed much more fuel on the journey making them uneconomical to operate.

Top: '**British Commerce**' was the first ship Ken served on. It was a 69,000 ton motor tanker built in 1965.

Above: '**British Confidence**' was the 68,000 ton steam turbine tanker built in 1965 that provided the inspiration for the Confidence name and livery.

My next telegram arrived: 'Join British Confidence, Hamburg'.

'British Confidence' was a sister ship to the 'British Commerce' and I thought it was a strange name. The Confidence, a 'C' class ship, was the same size as the Commerce except it was 'SS British Confidence' as opposed to 'MV British Commerce'. The MV standing for motor vessel whereas SS was a steam ship. This meant it had a steam turbine engine so there was more to learn.

This one also had engine problems (was it me?) resulting in us limping back from the Canary Islands to Falmouth, Cornwall for repairs. We enjoyed our week or so in Falmouth.

We eventually set off for the Gulf which took about three weeks going round Africa. In the Gulf we loaded the oil from derricks at sea which operated rather like oil rigs. Shortly after leaving to sail back around Africa we were informed to go to Portland, Maine, North America. It was a long journey with no land and I think we even went a week without seeing another ship.

At Portland the oil was sent by pipeline to Montréal as it was too cold for the ship to go to Canada with ice flows and the freezing of the St Lawrence River. It was our first time ashore for two months and the crew had not seen a member of the fairer sex for all that time! To put the timescale into perspective look at the date you are reading this, subtract two months, and think of all you have done and achieved in that time. These lads had spent all of that time on the ship. We were due to unload and leave the following day but as it turned out we had to stay longer as some crew members got blind drunk and arrested with others needing hospital treatment. I believe all of them had a good time.

Our next stop was Venezuela. On the journey down the east coast of America we went from freezing to warm seawater in a short distance when crossing into the Gulf Stream. That was a very busy watch. Seawater was used to cool the engines, plant and machinery and suddenly the change in temperature meant more coolant was needed so we spent most of the watch running around opening valves to maintain a constant temperature.

It was on this journey that we came across a small cabin cruiser drifting in the sea with two men aboard. They were waving their arms to attract our attention. We stopped but the captain would not let them board the ship as he was concerned about pirates. Being a bit green I thought that was mean because I had not seen any pirates or skull and crossbones and didn't even know modern-day pirates still existed. Anyway, we threw them a rope and the next thing there was a giant supertanker towing a tiny cabin cruiser with two blokes clinging on for dear life as the cabin cruiser bobbed up and down in the swell and commotion of the ship's propeller. We sailed very slowly and took them quite a long way, dropping them off at Aruba, an island in the Caribbean, 16 hours later. If they were pirates it served them right but, if not, then they were very lucky.

I did 6-7 months on 'SS British Confidence' before it was my time to leave. I enjoyed it much more than 'MV British Commerce' and being an officer (albeit junior) I had my own very nice cabin which was cleaned by one of the crew. All my food was supplied and wages were good so I was saving a lot of money, especially by my standards, and seeing places I would probably have never visited.

The next telegram arrived. This time it was 'British Bombardier' as Fourth Engineer so I had been promoted. Could I cope? I would have my own Junior Engineer which made me a bit nervous as I had not managed anyone before.

At this point you may enjoy a few tales. Can you stop a supertanker with jellyfish? 'British Bombardier' was another diesel ship but not quite as big as the other two. We were sailing along nicely when alarms started to ring – the engine temperature was up, so too the generator. It was all going off and I was starting to lose it. I rang the emergency bell for all engineers to come and help. I had to stop the engine and all the generators which caused a blackout. No power, just emergency lighting from batteries.

Lucky for me more senior engineers were more switched on. We had gone through a shoal of jellyfish – thousands of them – and sucked them into the filters which then became blocked preventing any cooling seawater reaching the critical points. We drifted for hours, shovelling hundreds of jellyfish from the filters. They were piled up in mountains around the engine room which was incredible. It took ages for them all to rot away – not to mention the smell!

A major mistake I made was I overlooked the freshwater tanks. We distilled our own water and had two tanks, one to use and one to top up. It was Christmas day (why did it have to be Christmas Day of all days?!) and the Captain, his wife and Chief Engineer were having drinks and needed water with the drinks. All of a sudden one of them said 'What's that bit of rust in the water?' 'Oh, and some more rust!' I got an angry phone call from the chef. I hadn't swapped the empty tank for the full one. It took a couple of days to clear the system and more than a couple of days for me to live it down.

One tropical afternoon on deck the Captain's wife was fishing. Harmless enough I thought, until she caught a big pufferfish. This strange fish, a bit like a multicoloured small football with a head and tail, was flapping around on the deck, breathing in and out, so one minute it was fully blown up, the next it went almost flat. No doubt the reason it is called a pufferfish. She saw me. '4 O' she called (4 O being 4th officer). 'Kill it, kill it' she screamed. Kill it? What was she thinking? I never even kill a fly let alone an angry pufferfish showing off all its capabilities. I got close to it. What do I do? Do I jump on it? Do I hit it?... I was a bit scared. Does it bite? Is it poisonous? Just in time a crew member came by, picked it up by its tail and swung it with full force against the bulkhead wall. With a load of hissing, it went just like a punctured tyre and was dead. She had it for her dinner.

This was to be my last ship. In just over two years I had achieved a fabulous experience, some savings, a suntan and grown up a bit. Wonderful.

I got married in January 1969 but only just made the wedding. 'British Bombardier' was sent to Finland with me still on it and we experienced some delays due to ice. The sea was freezing and so was the only bit of Finland that I saw. We returned to the Thames estuary and I was paid off. A coach belonging to Harris of Grays, Essex took me and others from the ship to the railway station where I caught a train to Leicester. With about three days to go before the wedding I had no time to buy a suit so I got married in uniform.

After the wedding we caught a couple of trains to Great Malvern where I had seen a lovely looking hotel on one of my Midland Red Day Anywhere excursions. I thought it was bound to be quiet at

One of the continental ports visited in 1966 was Lisbon, Portugal where Ken would have seen buses like this AEC Regent V LD2LA with locally built UTIC body. No 426 (HH-97-96) was new in November 1961 in a green and cream livery, changing to this orange and white scheme in the mid 1970s. It is now preserved in the UK. Simon Gill

the end of January. We found the hotel but have you ever heard of Robbie Burns? Lots of Scotsmen had – there was no room at the Inn! We trawled all over Malvern and eventually found a lifeless, quiet, cold, damp hotel. Two days later I was ill so we went home. Not a good start.

BRITISH TANKER COMPANY

On 28 May 1901, William Knox D'Arcy was granted a 60-year concession to search for oil and gas across most of Persia. (Iran). In 1909 he formed the **Anglo-Persian Oil Company** (APOC). The first shipment of crude oil left Abadan in April 1912 – bound for purchaser Royal Dutch-Shell.

British Tanker Company Limited (BTC) was the maritime transport arm of the Anglo-Persian Oil Company and was formed in 1915 with an initial fleet of seven oil tankers.

The **British Petroleum** brand was originally created by a German firm as a way of marketing its products in Britain. During the First World War the British government seized the company's assets, and in 1917 they were sold to Anglo-Persian. In 1924 the 'British Aviator' became the BTC's first diesel engine oil tanker, and was at that time the most powerful single-screw motor ship in the world. In 1935 the company was renamed **Anglo-Iranian Oil Company** (AIOC)

The fleet continued to grow in size and by 1939 had a fleet of 93 vessels. Unfortunately, 44 were lost during the Second World War.

After the war, the losses were replaced, ships grew in size and the first so-called 'super tankers' were built.

In November 1954, AIOC renamed itself the **British Petroleum Company**, and then became the **BP Tanker Company** from 1 June 1956.

Details of the three ships Ken served on are:

'**British Commerce**' was a motor tanker of 69,579 tons dwt (dead weight tons), built in 1965 by J L Thompson of Sunderland and scrapped in 1983.

'**British Confidence**' was a 67,944 ton dwt steam turbine tanker built by the well known Clydebank shipbuilders, John Brown & Co, in 1965 and scrapped in 1976. Both vessels were 815ft long with a 41ft draft.

'**British Bombardier**' was a steam turbine tanker built in 1962 by A Stephens of Glasgow, and was of 54,116 tons dwt. She was scrapped in 1976.

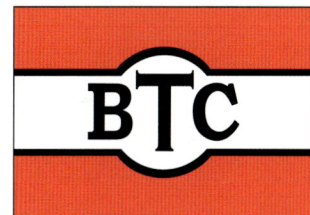

Chapter 5

The Fitter

Ken had a particular dislike of the ten AEC Bridgemasters as it was not easy to work on the engine. Leicester City Transport No 217 (217 AJF) was new in May 1971 with a Park Royal 76-seat body but only lasted in the fleet for ten years. After being found in a Glasgow scrap yard it has been fully restored and is seen recreating route 23 to Wigston Lane in Bowling Green Street, Leicester. Simon Gill

It was now back to buses. My thinking was, before I buy my own bus I had better practice on others. Back in 1969 there were two major bus companies in Leicester, Midland Red, which had just become part of the National Bus Company (NBC) and the Council owned Leicester City Transport (LCT). Midland Red's fleet was mostly home-made with not many buses getting a second life with another operator. LCT on the other hand had a fleet of AEC, Daimler and Leyland buses and these models would be far more likely to feature in my future plans so I applied for a job as a fitter.

The reply came – 'yes we have a vacancy in the Parks Department'. Oh no! 'If I can't work on buses then I'm not coming', was my reply. Thankfully, they created a space and I got a job in the bus fitting shop. It was Monday to Friday, a lot less money, but I grabbed the opportunity.

Comparing the different models was a bit unfair. The Leylands, especially the PD3s, were brilliant. The AECs were not Regent Vs, but Bridgemasters and Renowns. Strange choices in a city with no low bridge requirements and, because they were fewer in number, I never really mastered some of the basic jobs on them. You lifted

the bonnet lid and the engine seemed to be falling away and down towards the gearbox. The rocker cover nearest the gearbox had an oil bath on top and nine times out of ten, juggling it out of the confined space, I got a boot full of oil. This did not endear me to them and the Daimlers, again, were not standard having a David Brown gearbox which was troublesome.

I enjoyed working at LCT, with good people, some of whom I remain in contact with today. There were a few incidents during my time there. On one occasion I managed to drop a Gardner engine out of a Daimler without too much damage to the engine or anybody's feet – it bounced! I also managed to wedge a 36-foot long AEC Reliance in the door of the fitting shop. Luckily, we were able to move it eventually.

Another achievement was I learned to drive a bus, not as a PSV driver, but so I could take them out on road test. It was whilst working at LCT that I took my car driving test. I didn't have a car but I passed first time and then took up driving lessons on a double-decker bus with the Wallace School of Motoring based in Nottingham. I also passed at the first attempt driving a former Trent Leyland PD2.

I enjoyed the job but between BP Tankers and LCT I managed to get married and buy a house. I got the mortgage based on BP wages and I was now on a lot less, doing okay, but wanted to buy a bus.

Leicester had a lot of privately owned coach operators and there were still some privately run bus services. However, by this time none of the operators had double-deckers. I didn't know any of the people involved but after nearly 1½ years since starting at LCT it was time to buy my own bus.

But, how do you buy a bus and where from?

I used to read Commercial Motor magazine and there were dealers in Yorkshire, Cheshire, Bird's at Stratford-upon-Avon and Frank Cowley in Manchester and Dunchurch, Warwickshire. Not having a car I bought a Midland Red Day Anywhere ticket and went to Stratford-upon-Avon. I eventually found Bird's, but I don't think I made a very good impression as the chap I spoke to showed me a glimpse of some buses, but seemed to dismiss me as a time waster.

Walking back to Stratford I caught a bus to Rugby. I can't remember if it was one bus or I had to change at Leamington Spa, but belting along the A45 towards Rugby I saw the sign for Frank Cowley. I pressed the bell for the next bus stop and as I got off the driver looked at me. I am sure he was thinking why would anybody alight on the A45 in the middle of nowhere? I thank my lucky stars that I sat on the offside of the bus and saw the sign.

As I walked down the farm track that led from Frank Cowley's sign, only a few buses and coaches were in sight but the rear of a double-decker, PUF 647, caught my eye. I immediately thought it would be a Leyland Titan PD2 but it wasn't, it was a Guy Arab. The body was in very good condition. It was ex-Southdown from the Brighton and Portsmouth area, with a sliding cab door, unusual rear platform doors and posh seats. It was lovely but what about the Guy chassis? It had a Gardner engine, which was good – remember I had dropped one of those before and it survived. I recall they wanted £750 but this included a new Certificate of Fitness and they would paint it for me. That was a huge chunk out of my money but getting a Certificate of Fitness could be a nightmare and the repaint would be a great help.

Leicester London Road railway station is the location of Leicester City Transport No 40 (FJF 40D) an AEC Renown with East Lancs 74-seat body new in February 1966. Part of a batch of ten Renowns with unusual rear entrance bodies, it has been restored into the later LCT livery introduced in 1968 featuring a deeper cream and omitting the top crimson band.
Simon Gill

Ken's favourite buses in the Leicester fleet were the Leyland Titan PD3s. Here, No 90 (90 HBC), a PD3A/1 with East Lancs 74-seat body is seen in Uppingham Road. It was new in February 1964 and after spending twenty years with Bushey Middle School in South West London, where it took children to swimming lessons, it has been restored to original condition.
Simon Gill

The Certificate of Fitness (CoF) was a major test and examination of all buses and coaches. A bus would usually get a seven year CoF when it was new followed by a five year renewal. After that, the period would vary depending on the condition of the bus. The test entailed, amongst other things, crack testing, checking brakes, steering components and removing body panels to inspect the frame. It no longer takes place having been replaced by an annual MOT.

I didn't decide there and then but walked to Dunchurch where I caught a bus to Rugby, then another one from Rugby to Leicester, even managing to get back in time to watch Leicester City FC play an evening game. So, although the day has started badly it had got better.

The next week I went back to Dunchurch, again by bus, but this time taking a workmate from LCT with me for a second opinion.

We both walked from Dunchurch, along the A45, to Cowley's in the pouring rain. We got absolutely drenched and upon our arrival the salesman asked why we hadn't telephoned as he would have picked us up.

Anyway, the bus impressed us so I bought it. As you will recall, I didn't have a telephone in those days but he could send me a letter. He would arrange the new Certificate of Fitness and for it to be painted. What colour did I want? I knew red paint faded quickly and I wanted something that would only need doing once that was different to other buses. I was influenced by my career at BP. Ships don't get painted very often and black and grey can be quite attractive in certain light conditions and are very distinctive colours. The salesman said 'black and grey, are you sure?' 'Yes', I said, 'black and grey please'.

Chapter 6

The Owner

At the beginning of May 1970 I received a letter from Cowley's saying 'Your bus is ready'. My family took me to collect it in their new mini and followed me home. I remember the day very well as all the daisies were out and it was a great feeling to be driving my own bus.

I drove it home to Oadby and parked it on the drive of my house. It was a new house situated on a modern housing estate in a nice part of town. We all went inside for a cup of tea. I looked outside. Blimey it's big... had I really thought this out?

I couldn't settle as I felt uncomfortable thinking that curtains were twitching and I was upsetting the neighbours. It wasn't long before the neighbours' complaints started and sure enough, within a matter of days, a solicitors letter arrived telling me that large vehicles could not be parked at the house, neither could the house be used for the purpose of running a business. I moved 'PUF' onto some unused rough ground in King Street, Oadby. The street was not ideal so it was not long before I moved it to the lorry section of the main car park adjacent to Oadby Trinity Methodist Church off Harborough Road.

All I had to do now was find some passengers. Before I got a chance to do that I got a letter from the Ministry of Transport asking me to take my bus to the test station at Cannock Street, Leicester. Off I went, quite confident that with a new four-year Certificate of Fitness there would be no problems. I soon had the stuffing knocked out of me as 'PUF' failed and I was given a prohibition notice which stopped me from using it.

It was now back to Frank Cowley's who corrected the faults. On Monday, 18 May 1970 it was re-certified for four years. I then had to take the bus back to the test station where it was cleared and passed fit for service. That was a good wake-up call and, if anything, proved the importance of good maintenance. After hundreds of tests and only a few failures, we are still here today.

Surprisingly, when I look back, we got away with parking on what was commonly known as the Methodist Church car park for three

A newly repainted and certified PUF 647 is seen gleaming at the Clock Tower, Leicester in May 1970 with a young Ken Williams at the wheel. Fleet names and fleet numbers had not yet been applied. LCT 208 (XRY 208) a Leyland Titan PD3/1 with East Lancs body is on the left. Tom Moore

to four years, despite buying additional buses and coaches during that period.

I was finally ready to start business but where would I find those elusive passengers? During the first two months I only got about three jobs so, with money running out, there was no alternative but to advertise 'PUF' for sale. Just as the advert went in I won a school contract for one trip in the morning and one in the afternoon from Thurnby Lodge to Longslade School, Birstall. It was a start.

NEWS FLASH

18 MAY 1970

AT THE REQUEST OF PRIME MINISTER HAROLD WILSON, QUEEN ELIZABETH II ORDERED THE DISSOLUTION OF PARLIAMENT AND SET A DATE FOR A GENERAL ELECTION FOR THURSDAY, 18 JUNE 1970.

I decided to leave Leicester City Transport but as I wasn't earning enough money I got a part-time job at Brucciani's Coffee Shop during the midday rush, clearing and cleaning tables. This was good because I also got some dinner and a coffee and I was able to leave the bus near the city centre. Sadly, Brucciani's closed in May 2019 after 81 years of trading.

Things developed and in November 1971 I bought No 2, LDB 779, an AEC Reliance/Harrington coach from Nesbit Brothers of Somerby. It had been new to North Western Road Car Company, based at Stockport, and described as one of their finest post-war coaches. It had a red interior and had been

well liked by crews and passengers for over 10 years. It was also parked on Oadby car park – you could not do that today as cars struggle to find spaces, let alone lorries and buses.

An announcement in the local newspaper said a shoe firm was relocating. I contacted them and asked if they wanted a works bus. Yes they did, so I got a contract with High Cross Shoes which dovetailed nicely with Longslade School. I then got a contract to run a free bus service for shoppers to Brierley's Supermarket in Belgrave Gate. Frank Brierley was a pioneer 'stack 'em high; sell 'em cheap' shopkeeper who would stand on the stairs of his store with a microphone yelling out all the latest offers. A contract like that certainly helped to make the Confidence name more widely known.

I then gained some more school work and a contract with R Rowley & Co Ltd, a hosiery manufacturer, who had been running their own staff bus. After using a London RT for many years they had bought a former Southdown Leyland PD2/12 with East Lancs body, RUF 204, in August 1969. The bodywork was very similar in style to 'PUF' but the Leyland was not in the best of health. With all these new contracts we were finally away.

Christmas 1971 was not a good time. 'PUF' had developed knocking noises from the engine and I was having cylinder head gasket trouble with the AEC. On New Year's Day 1972 they were both off the road, not a great start to the New Year. The Guy had white metal bearings on the crankshaft that needed scraping in. It was a week of painstaking work, lying on the floor in the freezing cold, but everything was completed for the start of the new school term. It could have easily changed my mind about running buses but at least I got a new nickname 'Big End Ken'!

The AEC coach, No 2, always gave me head gasket or cooling problems. I remember doing a long weekend to Blackpool illuminations, going on Friday coming back on Sunday. The Friday was a freezing night and no heaters were working. It was a miserable journey and not one to win repeat business. In Blackpool the passengers bought vests, jumpers, coats, whiskey and boxes of matches for the return journey. I spent the Saturday trying to get rid of air locks in the heaters. On the return journey the heaters worked, it was boiling hot and the passengers were sweating. I was asked 'had I got any ice cream?'

Opposite page, top to bottom:

A rear view of Guy Arab IV/Park Royal No 1 (PUF 647) and Bedford SB1/Duple coach No 3 (456 FUP) on Oadby car park on 2 February 1974. The Trinity Methodist Church is in the background. Steve Smith

By the time this photograph was taken near the same spot in August 1974, the Guy had departed leaving Bedford SB1/Duple coach No 3 (456 FUP) alongside No 4 (XUF 845) a Leyland Titan PD3/4 with Northern Counties body. Simon Gill

The first site to be rented for parking was behind the Queen Victoria pub at High Street, Syston. Parked there on 4 March 1979 were No 4 (XUF 845) a 1959 Leyland Titan PD3/4 with Northern Counties body and No 7 (UOD 500) a 1957 Bristol Lodekka LD6B with Eastern Coach Works lowheight body. Ian Manning

This page, top to bottom:

A cold scene at Syston yard on New Year's Eve 1978 with, left to right, No 5 (749 DCD), No 7 (UOD 500) and No 4 (XUF 845). Steve Smith

The recently acquired yard at 30 Spalding Street, Leicester on 13 September 1980. The three fully visible vehicles are all ex-Southdown and from left to right are 5 (749 DCD) Leyland Leopard/Harrington, 9 (BUF 272C) and 4 (XUF 845) both Leyland Titan PD3/4s with Northern Counties bodies. The bus hiding behind the wall is 11 (GRY 55D). Steve Smith

A full yard five years later on 21 December 1985 shows, from left to right, coach 13 (AHA 451J) behind the wall, 11 (GRY 55D), 9 (BUF 272C) with 12 (HCD 356E) behind and red Routemaster 15 (WLT 655). Simon Gill

This page: **The recently acquired yard at Harrison Close, South Wigston on 1 November 1988 with Leyland PD3 No 9 (BUF 272C) being shielded by Leyland Atlantean No 16 (WTN 640H).** Simon Gill

Opposite page, top left to right: **Ground works for the workshop have started, bricks have been delivered and the first building is on the right. In the distance is Atlantean 16 boarded up as a shield to protect the other Atlanteans, all of which have Alexander bodies.** Ken Williams Collection

The building is up and the supporting brickwork for the vehicle ramp and pits is being completed. Ken Williams Collection

Roller shutter doors fitted and hardcore ready to start filling in the ramp up to the new pits inside the left hand door. Ken Williams Collection

Bottom left: **The pit has been completed and ex-Nottingham Leyland Atlantean/East Lancs No 27 (OTO 551M) is testing it out as the roller shutter door is being closed.** Ken Williams Collection

Bottom right: **No 27 again demonstrates there is lots of space to be able to work on the vehicles with a nice dry pit.** Ken Williams Collection

I started to get to know one or two local coach operators. One of them, County Travel, asked why I had an AEC and a Guy. He said I should have a Bedford as that was the little man's bus. Strangely enough he had one for sale and he said it was a good one, so I bought it in January 1973. 456 FUP became No 3 and replaced the AEC. It was the worst bus I ever ran. An electrical nightmare – the starter motor and dynamo fell off and when you put the lights on the heaters started. It was also horrible to drive which I likened to lying in a bath so, after two years, I sold it to local Bedford loving operator TRS Coaches. The owner later informed me it was a good coach. I thought, gosh, if that's a good one I'm glad I didn't have a bad one. It certainly lived up to being the little man's bus as, in my opinion, if you had too many of them you would never get big.

In August 1973 the next bus, No 4 came along. A former Southdown Leyland PD3 which had a similar chassis to those operated by Leicester City Transport that I loved. It replaced the Guy which was sold to a group of Southdown employees for preservation. They all came up to Leicester to collect it and take it back home to Brighton. The Guy still exists and is in superb condition, attending many rallies and events; even achieving stardom in the feature film 'Wish You Were Here' released in 1987.

In 1972 the president of Uganda, Idi Amin, expelled almost 60,000 Ugandan Asians from the country. The British government allowed 27,000 to move to the UK and many arrived in Leicester. Confidence gained some contracts taking their children from inner-city areas to suburban schools. We had buses taking people to work, children to school and then some of these children to overspill schools, both morning and afternoon. It was three trips in the morning and three trips in the afternoon and gave us a great boost.

With work picking up we needed a yard and some space. I was very conscious we couldn't continue with the public car park as we grew bigger. I can't remember the exact date but around 1975/76 I found a yard to rent at Syston. The downside was that it was 10 miles from home so I bought my first van. I had never had a car or van before, only my bike. I was 30 years old but 10 miles each way was a lot, before and after a long day, so the van became a necessity. We operated 4/5 buses from Syston yard which was located on High Street behind the Queen Victoria Public House.

I enquired about buying the former tram depot at 453 London Road, Leicester from Leicester City Council for use as a bus depot but could not get planning permission. At least it has now been saved by the Leicester Transport Heritage Trust for use as a small transport museum.

During 1979 an advertisement was spotted in the Leicester Mercury that a freehold transport yard was for sale at 30 Spalding Street, Leicester. I went to look at it and knew right away that I had to buy it. In my excitement, I have to admit that I drove through a red traffic light to get to the estate agent – that was, of course, in the van not a bus as that would never do. The estate agent quickly brought me back down to earth. Buying a property takes time and there are other interested parties! He asked 'have you got the money?' After protracted talks, visits to the bank manager and all the legals, it was eventually ours. This meant we could move out of Syston and the bonus was that it was nearer home. It was magic.

I needed to borrow money to make the purchase but, for the first time, a sense of security prevailed. Even better, we soon fixed up a fuel tank so no more visits to filling stations for diesel. I made it a priority to pay the loan off as quickly as possible and this was achieved well within the repayment schedule.

It wasn't long before Spalding Street was getting too small and an opportunity arose to rent some space from Miss Morley, owner of Provincial Garage, 115 Uppingham Road, Leicester. Provincial had been one of Leicester's foremost coach companies operating a sizeable fleet of mainly AEC coaches from a traditional coach garage, on routes to places like Southsea, for the Isle of Wight, and Coventry for the theatre. She sold her coach business to Barton in 1966.

Miss Morley told me she had space for two coaches, but no double-deckers. Her conditions were that we didn't get in her way; if we went out in the morning we could not return until late afternoon, the vehicles must not drop any oil on the floor and, most importantly, we didn't annoy the cats. There were lots of cats – some of them very grumpy. The former Midland Red Leyland Leopards, Nos 13 & 14, took up residence there and we kept to all the rules. Not sure how.

Then, in 1988 with parking space for buses still at a premium, we saw an advertisement for over half an acre of undeveloped land for industrial use for sale at Wigston. I got straight onto the estate agent who said 'Oh! I think it's already been sold'. The purchaser had said yes but was trying to get the land cheaper. The seller was fed up so I offered the full asking price. He said yes and I suspect the original purchaser who thought he had bought it was very disappointed.

Another visit to the bank manager, another loan, but again we paid the money back as quickly as possible. As and when we could afford it, we levelled the ground, put down hardcore and fenced off the land. We parked one bus on the site but it soon got smashed windows. We had some wooden screens made, which looked similar to sightscreens at cricket grounds, and surrounded the bus with these so the glass was not visible. This worked fine for a couple of months until a major storm smashed the screens and did more damage to the bus than the vandals.

A tree planting exercise took place to provide the site with some protection but it was obvious we needed a building so another trip to the bank manager for yet another loan. After architects, planners and builders we had, by 1990, a building erected for two buses. Good, but now I wish I had made it six feet longer as buses are bigger than they used to be. We also bought a second hand Portakabin.

Next, if I have remembered the terminology correctly, we had a design, plan and build workshop constructed. The pit has proved extremely useful – it was not dug down, as I have seen too many depots with pits full of water – so our buses drive up a ramp to enter the shed which also has two sets of vehicle lifts. Another Portakabin was also acquired for the drivers and we still had some space available.

Unfortunately, we still had visits from vandals and people stealing fuel from the fuel tank so, for some years now, we have employed 24-hour security. It's no fun watching people filling up 45 gallon barrels of your fuel on CCTV and police saying the picture is too grainy for them to use.

So, that's what we have achieved – two freehold depots, 24 old buses and an eventful existence.

Chapter 7

The Vehicles

Repainting buses took time during a busy schedule so was usually carried out during school holidays. No 4 (XUF 845) the first ex-Southdown Leyland Titan PD3, is seen at the bottom of High Street by the Clock Tower with lower panels repainted black but otherwise still in Southdown livery. Andrew Tucker Collection

It's not quite Paris but here is the Leyland Leopard/Harrington coach No 5 (749 DCD) on a day trip to Skegness on 20 August 1983. Adrian Rodgers

I have already touched on some of the vehicles Confidence has operated but a few more thoughts about them are appropriate.

When I first started, the price of the bus and its body condition were the most important. Most British chassis built in the early 1950s were very similar – usually very rugged and not susceptible to corrosion. I would not entertain any rare makes as spare parts are always required and they need to be easily obtained.

The Guy Arab was not a rare beast, certainly not in Birmingham, and the Park Royal body was quite lovely. Similarly, coach No 2, where the AEC Reliance was a common chassis and the Harrington coachwork very sturdy. However, its AEC AH470 engine was maybe not AEC's finest, being prone to cylinder head gasket problems.

Coach No 3, the Bedford/Duple was favoured by legions of small family owned coach operators the length and breadth of the country. It didn't work for me and was probably my worst buy, certainly in the early days.

Then came bus No 4. How lucky was I to obtain a Leyland Titan PD3 with doors at the front and quite a posh body. Southdown vehicles were always built and maintained to a very high standard and they sold them off quite young. The Leyland PD3 had been my favourite at LCT and, at last, I had got my own. It was fantastic. Once again, I bought it via the dealer, Frank Cowley and drove it back to Oadby on Friday, 31 August 1973. There was no time for a repaint as it was in use the following day carrying a party of primary school children. At that time, and for the next few years, repainting was carried out as and when time was available and the weather was suitable. By the end of October 1973 the green had been repainted black, but it retained cream window surrounds and roof for a while longer.

The next coach No 5 was a beautiful Leyland Leopard/Harrington. Once again, it was a former Southdown vehicle that served us well for over 10 years. It is the only vehicle that we have ever taken abroad on a trip to Paris.

If I could get them, Leylands were my favourites, but most double-deckers at that time had open rear platforms which were not the best for a school bus, so next came a couple of Bristol Lodekkas. They were very strong and sturdy and amongst the best quality built buses of the 1950s and 1960s. But where could you easily buy spare parts?

So, it was more or less Leyland from then onwards. The PD3 with air brakes was a fabulous bus as was the Leopard for both bus and coach use. I was aware of some operators not favouring Leopards because they felt the brakes were not very efficient but it was not a problem for us. I heard lots of tales of near misses and hair raising descents of steep hills. The fleet therefore became all Leyland from 1980 onwards with several PD3s and Leopards following on. We painted a former LCT PD3, No 11, at Astill & Jordan's depot at Ratby in August 1980 whilst the rear doors were being fitted. This was the first bus to receive red lining out to complement the black and grey livery. This quickly became the new standard.

The first bus to receive red lining out to separate the grey and black livery was ex-Leicester Leyland PD3/Metro-Cammell No 11 (GRY 55D). It is seen on an enthusiasts' excursion in Coalville on 5 June 1993. Simon Gill

As the supply of PD3s dried up the choice narrowed down to either the Leyland Atlantean or Daimler Fleetline. In my view, the Leyland chassis was better than the Fleetline, but on early PDR models the fluid flywheel was a weakness. I had experienced these at LCT where a batch of 20 delivered in 1968/69 had constant transmission problems. After these difficulties LCT never bought another Leyland double-decker. I only bought one Leyland Atlantean PDR type, No 16, which was done hastily to replace accident damaged PD3 No 10. It was a beast.

It quickly became apparent to me that if I had a good bus it might be old, but it was better than a troublesome more modern one, and that still applies to this day.

I briefly considered buying the three Tyne & Wear PTE pre-production Volvo Ailsas with Alexander bodies (GCN 1-3N) as these had engines at the front, next to the driver, as well as a front entrance with doors so would have been ideal. I decided against it as they had only lasted three years with the PTE and had unusual hydraulic brakes.

A day out in London, as a tourist, enabled me to travel on several AEC Routemasters. I was very impressed; some of them even had Leyland O.600 engines which were the same as those fitted in the PD3. The first ones were being withdrawn and I was aware that the Leyland version was not London's favourite. I wanted Leyland engines and CAV electrics, whereas most Routemasters had AEC engines and many had Sims electrics. Sims had not long been acquired by CAV so I foresaw problems ahead with Sims. In 1985/86 I bought two Leyland/CAV equipped Routemasters and No 15 is still with us and is lovely for a wedding or special occasion.

It was now back to Leyland and the first Atlantean AN68s, Nos 18/19 from Southport were beautiful. The AN68 had much improved transmission over the earlier PDR example. Next came Nottingham City Transport OTO 540M; an early casualty in the NCT fleet due to engine failure. I was allowed to buy it provided I paid for a reconditioned engine and the fitting charges. Nottingham style bodies where unusual but well engineered using lots of common parts, so No 20 entered the fleet. It was so good we had eight more over the next few years.

AN68s also came from Portsmouth City Transport, which had just been taken over by Stagecoach, and was another splendid fleet. All these buses were superb, the Nottingham ones even having a simple rotary fuel pump. Then, as always, things started to change as, in the quest for improvement, cost savings and efficiency, sulphur was removed from diesel fuel. It was the sulphur in the fuel that lubricated the rotary pumps. They ran okay in cool weather but I remember one hot afternoon when the telephone never stopped ringing. Drivers were experiencing breakdowns all over the city. The only cure was to wait and let the engines cool down which was not good for passenger satisfaction, driver's patience or my blood pressure.

On the coach side of the business we stayed with Leyland Leopards and Tigers. The Tiger was brilliant with semi-automatic transmission but a horror with a manual gearbox. We had one,

No 43, a lovely coach, bought quite cheaply at an auction. It was horrendous. Nobody could drive it, including me.

I remember taking a load of Army squaddies to Stanstead airport. I was pleased to get onto the A14 but, near Cambridge, horror of horrors, the road was closed due to an accident and we were diverted around lots of country lanes. Every time I changed gear I never knew if I had got a higher gear or a lower one, or even the same one I had been in, so we had a journey of kangaroo jumps when the gear was too high or sudden lurches, to almost a stop, if the gear was too low. I'm sure 50 squaddies wondered why I was in the driving seat, all of them thinking they could have done better. At Stanstead I had to go on the runway to take them to their plane; I just hope their pilot was better with his aeroplane than I had been with No 43. Luckily, I drove back to Leicester empty, still getting the gears wrong but at least nobody was tutting. I had a well-deserved pint that night.

Next came the Leyland Olympians. Surely the best double-decker bus ever built from an operator point of view. We have had 22 from various operators and we still have six now, some of them 38 years old. Far better, more reliable and cheaper to run than any previous or subsequent buses. A depot full of Leyland Olympians and semi-automatic Leyland Tigers was utopia. Engineers and schedulers had plenty of sleep and life was good – but I don't think we knew that at the time.

Leyland was acquired by Volvo. The Volvo B10M, especially an automatic one, was a superb single deck bus and coach. The first one with Van Hool body, No 40, introduced the new red and black coach livery in 1999, which I based on my beloved Midland Red.

Even the Volvo D10M Citybus, using the same basic chassis, was great, but the double deck body was lower to the road. This was fine if kept on regular routes but, as we found out with No 74, ground clearance became a major problem if it strayed from main roads. At 14ft 10ins high it hit lots of trees the other buses missed; especially the Leyland Olympians with ECW bodies being 1ft 2ins lower. Road humps were also a problem for No 74, so it was not a 'go anywhere' bus.

Volvo took over the Olympian and their version was a good bus, but the chassis was made of much thinner metal so I don't think many will reach 38 years in service. So, after all these purchases what did I buy next?

Well, I went mad. It was 2008, we were doing well, I was wearing rose tinted spectacles, felt I had worked hard, the buses had done okay and I wanted to put something back into the bus industry. Let's buy a brand new bus… but how do you buy a brand new bus? There were dealers who sold brand new coaches, some of which were based in Leicestershire, but a brand new double-decker bus… I wasn't aware of any dealer that could help. Ever since the early 1960s I had visited Earls Court for the Commercial Motor Show and I also made a couple of visits to Kelvin Hall, Glasgow for the Scottish Motor Show. In 1978, the Trade shows moved to the NEC Birmingham and I still make an annual pilgrimage.

The Leyland Olympian has been the preferred choice of double-decker for the past 20 years. A typical example with lowheight Eastern Coach Works body is no 51 (EEH 903Y) which was originally new to Midland Red (North) of Cannock, Staffordshire. It was running an enthusiasts' tour when seen at St. Margaret's bus station on 16 May 2009. Simon Gill

Confidence introduced a new coach livery from 1999 which was inspired by the red and black used by Midland Red. It is shown to good effect on this preserved BMMO C5 with Carlyle 37-seat body, both built by the operator in March 1959. It was Midland Red 4780 (780 GHA). This type of coach introduced motorway express services when the M1 opened that year, allegedly travelling at speeds in excess of 80 mph. This was in the days before a speed limit was introduced. Simon Gill

Over the years, I had got to know some salesmen, especially those at Leyland, which had become Volvo and East Lancs Coachbuilders. I must explain that at this time it was common to buy two products. One manufacturer built the chassis, e.g. the bones, with the wheels and the engine. Well known names included Volvo, Dennis and Scania. Another company built the body; in other words, the bits you see and feel.

I wrote to two or three manufacturers of chassis and bodies and only got one reply from East Lancs. For many years at the trade shows I had joked with the East Lancs salesmen that I was looking at their products so I would know what to buy in 20 years' time when they became second-hand. Most bus manufacturers wanted orders for batches of buses, not just one, but East Lancs were very obliging, didn't take the 'mickey' and could also procure the chassis. 'Could I have one of your bodies on a Volvo?' 'Yes, I could', they said and it would cost £189,000. Wow! That didn't leave a lot of money left but we did it. A brand new Volvo B9TL with an Olympus body arrived in the December. It was given fleet number 71, with cherished number plate FJ58 CON. What a beauty! I was very proud. It was ideal for private hire, especially for trips to London.

The following year I bought a former Stagecoach London Dennis Trident which became No 72. A lovely bus to look at and ride on but, believe it or not, it has an engine fitted the wrong way round into the narrowest of gaps, making the fuel pump, pipes and all the bits that give trouble at the back of the engine, totally inaccessible. In addition, it has a gearbox that does not like going backwards

Arriving at Wollaton Park, Nottingham on 31 May 2009 is the six month old Volvo B9TL with Optare Olympus body – the first and only new bus bought by Confidence. Its full story may be found in Part 2 of this book. Simon Gill

and, compared to everything else we had at the time, horrendous fuel economy. No more of these will be purchased.

Since the demise of bus conductors, buses seldom reverse. All routes tend to go 'round the block' at the terminus and reverse is only used in depots and some bus stations. If you don't believe me, watch some 1990s buses reversing over the humps at your local bus station – they can hardly do it. We serve schools, many of which are at the end of a cul-de-sac with some at the top of a hill. Just watch the net curtains twitching when the bus is screaming away in reverse going at about half a mile an hour, climbing the hill backwards.

Three years later I acquired our first Volvo B7TL. Much better, but still very poor fuel economy and a far more complicated bus than had gone before. Not only that, but on all these ex-London buses we had to remove the middle door, fit extra seats, rebuild the floor, remove the wheelchair fittings and alter the electrics. At that time I had no idea the Public Service Vehicles Accessibility Regulations 2000 (PSVAR) would apply to us. So far, of the low floor buses, the Volvo B7TL has been our favourite. I have also tried a couple of DAF DB250s, but spare parts are very expensive and they are not very common unless part of an Arriva fleet.

In the future I envisage Volvo chassis, mostly double deck, with not much prospect for a coach fleet. With constant changes in the law a non-PSVAR coach is not much good now and, if you want to go into many city centres, a Euro 6 engine is the minimum requirement. How long will it be before we need Euro 7 or electric engines? Will we buy PSVAR single deck buses? At this stage I honestly don't know. Even fitting seat belts to more modern buses is not as straightforward as it has been previously, again due to new laws and legislation. It doesn't get any easier running buses!

Chapter 8

The Experiences

I decided quite early on that we would concentrate on being a bus operator and did not want to run coaches except on local schools and UK private hire work. At around the time I bought the Bedford, I visited County Travel. Whilst waiting to see the owner I could not help overhear a girl in the office on the telephone speaking to a theatre in Paris. The conversation was partly in English and partly in French. She was trying to change some tickets as their passengers had changed their minds about which show they wanted to see. I could tell she was struggling so I was determined I never wanted to have that hassle.

We do quite a lot of bus hire taking mourners to funerals. A lot of people, unfamiliar with Leicester, arrive at the deceased's house and then have the option of travelling on the bus to go to the crematorium and return, or making their own way.

Most of our buses are painted the same and can be seen all around the city especially on school days. On one occasion, several motorists decided to make their own way. Keeping up and following a bus in city traffic, with all the traffic lights and junctions, is not easy. The funeral bus set off with a convoy of cars behind. Travelling along Humberstone Road a Confidence school bus left Spence Street swimming baths to go to Charnwood primary school in Highfields. This involves an intricate manoeuvre turning round up a dead-end to avoid low bridges. On this occasion, the school bus was surrounded by cars and couldn't turn round. The funeral cortege had seen two Confidence buses and mistakenly followed the wrong one.

Once, on a school sports team bus the girls came back first. Some of the girls started talking to me, chatting about various things. Suddenly, one said, 'I'd like a boyfriend like you.' I thought watch out, then she said, 'but without the wrinkles.' Phew.

Talking to a boy at a Catholic school before the afternoon return journey, I asked him what he had learnt that day. 'Oooh' he said, 'I had sex education'. I said 'I didn't think Catholic schools taught sex education' to which he replied, 'Oh no, not in school, it was in the playground at dinnertime!'

As you can probably gather, we have done quite a lot of school work over the years and some schools have unusual names, but you get familiar with them as they become part of the daily language. One day, we went away on holiday and my dad came over to stand in answering the telephone. On one such call the voice on the other end of the telephone said 'Can you help me? This is Judgemeadow'. 'Oh! If I can your honour' my dad replied. Judgemeadow is the name of a local school!

It wasn't only children who got up to mischief; I remember carrying a bus full of male passengers on 'PUF' who had had a lot to drink. We were on a motorway when they needed the toilet and I couldn't stop. We had just passed the exit for a junction so they decided to stand on the back platform, open the doors and let go, just as cars came down the adjacent slip road to join the motorway. It was otherwise dry and I remember seeing gushing liquid in my near side mirror and the windscreen wipers coming on, on a car, as it passed me.

The Leyland PD3s went to the East Coast as well as London and seen in Mablethorpe on 21 August 1986 are ex-Southdown No 12 (HCD 356E) and No 9 (BUF 272C). Adrian Rodgers

The members of one Working Men's Club were a bit lively and got up to several tricks. The last ¾ mile home was along a dual carriageway and was quite open with cycle paths. They almost always stopped me before this open stretch of road and threw somebody off the bus who they had stripped naked. I then had to drive off and the unlucky person had to streak home. We once had a police escort all the way back from Skegness and, on another occasion, we were stopped by the police to retrieve a stolen bicycle found in the coach boot.

Once, taking a church group out for the day, we'd only just started off when the organiser ordered me to stop in a very busy section of road. The organiser said 'we must do the rosary' so there we were stopped, blocking up the road and causing havoc, whilst they all said their prayers for a safe journey.

On another occasion I recall taking school children from Longslade School to Glenfield. The front of the school was being rebuilt and travelling along Groby Road one of the children dropped a half brick from the top deck window which incredibly landed on the passenger seat of an open top sports car overtaking us. Not a happy driver.

I drove a Leyland PD3 to London once via the M1 motorway. It was a private hire requiring a double-decker and we stopped at Toddington Services amongst all the smart shiny coaches for a break. As the time came to leave, two girls came up to me (because they knew I was the driver) and said 'which is our bus?!'

Our first venture into running a bus service was the 45 service from the University of Leicester to the halls of residence near Oadby. It was initially won on tender and began on Monday 6 October 1986, the first journey operated by AEC Routemaster

Monday 6 October 1986 saw the launch of the first stage carriage service by Confidence. Route 45 connected the halls of residence near Oadby with the University of Leicester. Here on arrival at the University on the very first trip is No 15 (WLT 655), the 1961 AEC Routemaster with Park Royal body. Simon Gill

The second journey on that Monday morning was operated by the 1967 Leyland PD3/Northern Counties No 12 (HCD 356E). It is seen arriving at the University on its first trip with a full load. Destination blinds were not fitted at first so a board was used which can be seen on the front between the registration number and radiator grille. Simon Gill

No 15 (WLT 655) arriving at the University at 9.15am. The two AEC Routemasters were ideal for this service which we began running commercially three weeks later following the introduction of deregulation on 26 October 1986. The two mile journey was often full with a standing load of passengers. I was conducting on one occasion and you know it is going to be a bad trip when the first passenger you serve offers a pound coin for what was, I think, a 32p fare. I collected all the lower deck fares and went upstairs to the full top deck. Panic set in; there was only ¼ mile to go so how was I going to collect all those fares?

I started at the back then, horror of horrors, the aluminium cover over the roll of tickets fell off the front of my Setright ticket machine. Sounding like a bell as it hit the floor, it attracted lots of attention

and as I bent down to pick it up the ticket roll came off the spindle and rolled down the aisle in a straight line to the front of the top deck. It left me with an unbroken length of ticket from my machine, strapped around me at the back of the bus, with the remainder of the roll on the floor at the front. I chased after it but, on bending down to pick it up, the money fell out of my leather cash bag all over the floor. The student passengers were in uproar, laughing and cheering and I was left very embarrassed and red-faced with coins all over the floor and passengers getting off having had the most entertaining free bus ride in years.

A wonderful day on another occasion involved a private hire for a group who were going cockling and shrimping at Fosdyke Wash in Lincolnshire. The only problem was on the return journey I had mountains of cockles with a short shelf life but no fridge.

Fishing clubs are not always fun. Getting up at 4:30am on a cold and frosty Sunday morning and then driving out to some godforsaken stretch of water in the middle of nowhere in the Lincolnshire Fens. The passengers got off the coach at a remote footpath and disappeared into the murky mist, crunching on the ice, loaded up with fishing rods, baskets, maggots… maggots, don't talk to me about maggots!. I was left parked up for 6½ hours with no shops and heating that lasted about 6½ minutes! Oh! How I dreaded those jobs, but I needed the money.

Bus No 8 (273 AUF), a former Southdown Leyland Leopard, went to Dudley. In those days the former Midland Red Dudley depot had some rough ground on the opposite side of the road in Birmingham Road. Our driver parked up alongside the other buses and went for a walk. When he returned the bus had had a full interior clean thanks to the West Midlands PTE depot cleaner.

Trips to the seaside were usually enjoyable but I used to worry in case anything went wrong. A convoy of three Leyland PD3s and coach No 5 (749 DCD) had a job to Skegness and back. The journey there went well and we all had a good day in the sunshine with a walk along the promenade and fish and chips.

It was time to go home. All the vehicles started okay, no children had been lost, everyone was alive and there were no injuries. We got to Grantham, all in a row, with me at the back. Climbing out of Grantham through Harlaxton everything was fine. We got to the big climb on the A607 and just before we arrived at the summit the front bus stopped on a very steep incline, so we all stopped. Oh dear, what's happened? I got out the cab and ran to the front bus. The driver, an Irishman, was standing bent up in the cab. I leaned in and shouted, 'what's up Bob'. In his stuttering Irish accent he informed me that his seat had collapsed and it was flat on the cab floor. 'How did that happen' I enquired, trying not to appear panicked. Apparently, he was trying to adjust it whilst we were going so slowly and had wound it off the top of the thread, causing it to collapse. Mild panic changed to relief as it was not engine failure. We got him out of the cab, refitted the driver's seat, adjusted it and carried on the journey. Only Bob could drive his bus all the way from Leicester to Skegness and half way back again before trying to adjust his seat on the longest, steepest hill of the journey.

Another driver, Joe, came from Black & White, Cheltenham. He was used to driving fast coaches but he didn't last long as our buses were too slow, especially the Bristol Lodekka's. He said they spoilt his driving.

Chapter 9

The Ups and Downs

There have been many 'ups' over the years and they have already been covered. Most relate to significant purchases like the first bus, No 1, Leopard coach No 5, not to mention purchasing the depots at Spalding Street and Harrison Close, Wigston. There was also, of course, brand new bus No 71 which briefly brought new energy and enthusiasm to the business.

It should have started an exciting time for us but it arrived in December 2008 just as the financial crisis hit the UK. Leicestershire County Council, who was our biggest customer, started to cut back so that we only undertake a very small amount of work for them now. Schools started to become Academies from 2010 and Government cut backs began to bite, not to mention all the other bureaucracy bus operators have had to endure over the past 11 years.

A major blow came in 2012 when two very trusted employees embezzled over £70,000 from the company. It took a lot to recover and it was a good job everything was paid for and we had no debt.

One of the pair bought his own bus and started up in competition with us, effectively using money he had stolen from us which he later admitted in court. He knew all our clients and that really hurt. Other misdemeanours followed and he ended up with a jail sentence. It was so sad.

In June 2018 the new Volvo B9TL, No 71, was lost in a fire. It had just returned from a private hire to a stately home in Northamptonshire and dropped off the passengers at a school close to our Wigston depot. A warning light came on in the cab. The regular driver, who was very familiar with the bus, thought it was strange so decided to go straight back to the depot before his next trip. Sadly, the bus didn't make it and burst into flames just before the depot. It was later diagnosed as an electrical fault around the alternator. It was another big blow, as is the increase in insurance premiums ever since – the insurance company sold No 71 for scrap.

The only new bus bought by Confidence, No 71 (FJ58 CON) was lost in a fire caused by an electrical fault in June 2018. A sad end to a fine vehicle. Simon Gill

The Future

We live in changing times where policies and the way of life are vastly different to when we started. In the 1970s all local transport requirements for schools in the city of Leicester were supplied by council owned Leicester City Transport. That included all trips to swimming baths, playing fields and home to school journeys. Any LCT could not do they passed on. In Leicestershire, journeys were tendered through the County Council.

Later, Government changes meant that there was no longer an obligation for Councils to provide free swimming lessons and if schools still wanted to continue with them they had to pay for both hiring the baths and the bus. Slowly, we gained more of this work.

In October 1986 deregulation of bus services began, whereby any legal licensed bus company could do commercial bus service work. Confidence was tempted by deregulation but it was better picking up school swimming contracts whilst the other companies battled it out on bus service work. The swimming and playing field runs at this time fitted in well between our school contracts.

Deregulation in Leicester produced winners and losers. It largely depended on what you wanted. A trend by some small operators was to attack the big boys, be a nuisance and get bought out. One enterprising firm did this three times and his name is still in use. Another did it twice. However, I wanted to be there long-term with stability. I was not too bothered about getting rich quickly.

I always knew there was little real money in running buses. If we attacked Leicester CityBus (which LCT had become), Midland Fox (successor to Midland Red) or Trent, we wouldn't win. I have never believed in 'David and Goliath'. In fact, we ended up doing Sunday bus services and a bingo run for Leicester CityBus, whilst they fried bigger fish.

All of the small Leicester firms who ran bus services in the 1980s have gone, including the old traditional firms that operated services before deregulation. Some set seeds for larger groups whilst some left the industry altogether, with money in their pockets.

Confidence carried on undertaking school work and private hire, keeping, I think, good relations with the big boys. I like to think that children can't drive so schools are a good market. Unfortunately, I didn't foresee parents having two cars, driving their children everywhere and then buying them their own cars on their 17th birthday. Nor did I ever foresee schools being changed into Academies or Free Schools. Parents now have a choice so not all the children in the same street go to the same school; they go all over the place. This eliminates major flows of passengers, therefore making it difficult to cater for with buses, so parents or even children themselves, drive back and forth to school. As I write this there appears little hope for reducing traffic congestion and pollution in the short-term.

Another change that is difficult to manage is that senior schools now finish the day earlier, some at 2.45pm. Primary schools still

One of the Sunday bus services picked up from Leicester CityBus was the 10/11 Inner Link. AEC Routemaster No 15 (WLT 655) is seen on route 11 in Queens Road, Clarendon Park heading to Evington Valley Road on Sunday 24 June 1990, by which time full use was being made of the destination indicators. Simon Gill

finish around 3.20pm / 3.30pm. Senior schools are most likely to produce potential bus passengers whereas primary schools go swimming, so the jigsaw no longer fits. Sometimes, two buses and two drivers (which can be hard to find) are required when one used to do the job nicely. This is not good for the bottom line.

Recently, I carried some children from an outlying village school into Leicester. They wanted to know what the press buttons were for on the seat stanchions. When told, the next question was 'why do you want a bell?' Children in places like Leicestershire never go on a bus or train if they are with their family, so how on earth can they get hooked on public transport? Perhaps the climate change debate will alter their opinion and they will put pressure on their parents to change behaviour.

I sometimes wonder if we will actually make it to our 50th anniversary. In late October 2019 there was comment within the bus and coach industry that the new PSVAR rules would include school contracts. I thought surely not. I fully understood that PSVAR applied to registered bus services from 1 January 2020 but as our school runs are a private arrangement between a school and us, it was one of the main reasons none has been registered as I thought we would be exempt.

The main reason other operators registered school contracts was to claim fuel duty rebate. Many of our runs are quite short so I didn't want to commit to going to and from schools at set times and routes as we vary slightly every day especially when arriving at a school in the afternoon. The cost of claiming would probably outweigh the benefits.

It came to light that school contracts are included in PSVAR unless pupils travel free of charge. In 2005, when they announced PSVAR applied to registered services, school transport was free. In the meantime Government policy towards schools has quietly changed and funding cuts have stopped free transport for the over 16's. One way or another, Academies probably charge pupils to travel and the few remaining County Council school runs now carry fare paying passengers. Hence the reason the new regulations slipped under the radar.

So, school contract buses and coaches need to incorporate features to enable disabled people to travel on them comfortably and safely, including a wheelchair space and a ramp or lift. This means, for example, bell pushes have to be palm operated and within a metre of each seat together with all the other requirements of the Act.

For a small operator like us this is a disaster causing more sleepless nights. For several years we have been converting PSVAR buses to make them more suitable for use on school work by removing centre doors, adding extra seats and rebuilding floors, all of which has cost a lot of time and money. As I write this the Department for Transport has agreed to grant a temporary exemption until 31 July 2020 to give small operators like us more time to consider the way forward.

Many other small operators have spent a fortune on lovely brand new coaches, most of which get cascaded down for use as school coaches, none of which is PSVAR compliant. There are brand new coaches out there worth £300,000+ that do not have wheelchair access. How much are they worth now? How did all this slip by the manufacturers, the dealers and the operators?

The first second-hand low floor bus I bought was this ex-Stagecoach London Dennis Trident 2 with Alexander ALX400 body. It was converted from dual to single door to ensure the safety of children and so we could get more seats on the lower deck. No 72 (V125 MEV) is on home to school run SP2 between Glen Parva and St Pauls School, Evington.
Adrian Rodgers

The main dealer in ex-London buses has converted hundreds for school use but what good are 18 seats on the lower deck of a double-deck school bus? If we all knew, would we have bothered? Now, suddenly, any 2005 PSVAR equipped bus is worth £20,000 more than it was in October 2019, regardless of make or type. In my view this means even totally unreliable models with inaccessible engines, difficult parts availability and horrendous fuel consumption figures are now more valuable than good, reliable work horses which are suddenly of little value and destined for the scrap yard or export.

It gets worse. With the exception of London very few bus operators dispose of buses younger than 15 years old so you can't just go out and buy a second hand fleet; they simply don't exist. It seems to me that these new rules have been drawn up by someone in a leafy suburb who drives their children to school. I am not sure the same applies to inner city Leicester.

Who, in their right mind, would buy a bus costing £200,000+ to do a school contract for 190 days a year when they only receive, in Leicester anyway, about £180 a day? The economics do not add up.

As I climb down from my soapbox let us all enjoy looking back at the previous 49⅔ years whilst we limp into our 50 years celebration. We will endeavour to continue but will never be 'Coach Operator of the Year'. We try to buy the right vehicles for our needs and keep them a long time and in good condition. Don't forget the engineering side to running buses is crucial and cannot be skimped.

I would like to pay tribute to everyone who has worked for Confidence, both now and in the past, as without them we would be nowhere. We try to keep stable, almost boring, but hopefully continue to keep our customers and local transport enthusiasts happy, of which I am proud to be one.

Remember, it's not just any old school bus – it's the Cᴏɴꜰɪᴅᴇɴᴄᴇ school bus!

PART TWO

THE FLEET

ROUTEMASTER

The Fleet in Detail

Introduction

Many of the buses and coaches operated by Confidence have an interesting history so if you want to know more about the vehicles you have travelled on, what happened to them, or are just interested in the ones operated by the company, we hope to answer your questions.

These details are based on information from various sources and great care has gone into ensuring they are as complete and accurate as possible. However, we have to rely on what has been recorded by others and some dates may vary slightly. If you can provide more accurate information then please let us know. There are two sets of information:

1. An in depth history of each vehicle together with photos.
2. Fleet Summary giving basic details of all 90 vehicles operated and those acquired for spares or on loan.

Layout of Information

The format of the detailed history of each vehicle is as follows:

Fleet Number	Registration Number	Chassis make and type	Chassis Number	Seating Capacity
		Body make and type	Body Number	
Date	Operator and other details such as changes to the vehicle, seating arrangement, registration number etc.			
Denotes when the vehicle entered the Confidence fleet.				

The details have been grouped together by vehicle type to make identification easier. The seating arrangement follows long established practice used by historians which describes the type of vehicle and seating capacity. Those used are:

Prior to the figures
B   Single deck bus
C   Coach
H   Double deck bus with centre gangway on both decks
DPH Double deck bus built to semi-coach standards
FH   Double deck bus with a front mounted radiator concealed by a full front

The figures indicate the number of seats with the upper deck capacity shown first followed by the lower deck.

After the figures
F   Entrance is at, or towards the front and doors are fitted
FT   Front entrance as above but a toilet is also fitted
D   Doors at the front and in the centre
R   Rear entrance with open platform
RD   Rear entrance fitted with doors

As an example, a description of FH39/30F means a double deck bus with a front mounted radiator concealed by a full front, with 39 seats on the upper deck and 30 seats on the lower deck and an entrance at, or towards the front, with doors fitted.

Where previous or subsequent owners are shown these may not always show if a vehicle has passed through a dealer as these details are not always recorded. Only those that we are aware of have been included.

Some vehicles have been broken up for spares and their remains scrapped on site – usually at Wigston depot. Not all details of subsequent scrap dealers are known.

Photographs of every vehicle, including some when with previous or subsequent operators, are included. We have tried to show Confidence vehicles in a variety of locations but the very nature of the operations mean some of them are regularly seen in the same places and inevitably, some have been taken at depots.

Fleet Summary

Confidence has only used one chronological fleet number system so every vehicle is listed in fleet number order which, with very few exceptions, is the order they entered service.

This is followed by the registration number that applied whilst in service with Confidence, then the chassis make, body make, seating arrangement, year the vehicle was new, when it was acquired by Confidence and finally, its disposal date. 'Current' means the vehicle was part of the fleet when this book was compiled.

Company name:	**CONFIDENCE BUS AND COACH HIRE LIMITED**		
Current licence:	PF1018051 (Incorporated on 7 February 2003)		
Previous licence:	PF0007078 (Surrendered in May 2003 – K M Williams T/A Confidence Coaches)		
Depots	1. 30 Spalding Street, Leicester, LE5 4PH. Vehicle Authorisation: 6 vehicles		
	2. 10 Harrison Close, South Wigston, LE18 4ZL. Vehicle Authorisation: 21 vehicles		
Liveries			
Current liveries	Buses	Black and Light Admiralty Grey with Red lining	
	Coaches	Currently varies but usually all over Grey / Silver except	
		No 80 is Red with Black skirt and Grey panels below window level	
		No 89 is Metallic Blue with a Silver band	
Previous liveries	Coaches	Red with Black window surrounds and roof; Admiralty Light Grey with a Black skirt	

Opposite page: **The Routemaster badge on the front grille of No 15 (WLT 655).**

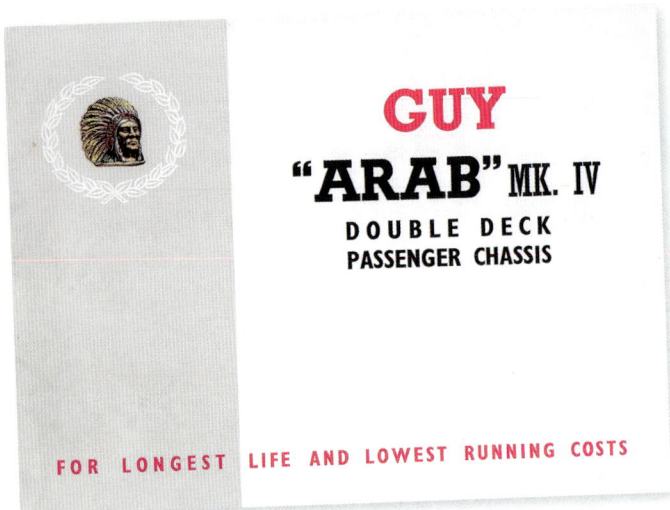

Guy 'Arab' IV Sales Brochure dated September 1956.

Two pages from the Guy Arab IV Sales Brochure showing the chassis arrangement and different operators specifications.

Guy Arab

The Guy Arab was a popular chassis with many operators who had been forced to buy them during the Second World War when new chassis were not available. The Mark IV was introduced following a large order for Birmingham City Transport in 1950. Most were fitted with concealed 'New Look' radiators but Southdown retained exposed radiators to cool the popular Gardner 6LW, 8.4 litre engine.

During its service with Southdown it had latterly operated in the Brighton area and was unique as the only Guy Arab IV delivered to Southdown with a two-piece 'Southlanco' sliding door. All the others had four-piece 'jack-knife' doors.

The 'Southlanco' door was designed by Alfred Alcock of East Lancashire Coachbuilders to prevent sliding doors on rear entrance buses hitting the rear wheel arch. It was made in two sections that ran on two separate sets of tracks. By using two different sizes of gear wheel on the motor shaft the inner leaf, which extended to the rear of the platform, travelled at twice the speed of the outer leaf. This enabled them both to reach the open and closed positions simultaneously.

With fleet No 1, this was the first bus acquired by Ken Williams, entering service in May 1970. It was collected for preservation on Sunday 31 March 1974 and has been restored in Southdown livery, regularly attending events in the south of England.

1	PUF 647	Guy Arab IV (6LW)	FD72880	H33/26RD
		Park Royal	B38420	
	May 1956	New to Southdown Motor Services No 547		
	Jan 1970	Sold to Frank Cowley Ltd (dealer), Dunchurch, Warwickshire		
	May 1970	**Confidence, Oadby, Leicester**		
	Mar 1974	Bus Interest Group, Brighton for preservation		
	1992	David Morgan, Nutfield, Surrey for continued preservation		

With fleet No '1' set in the destination indicator, PUF 647 is seen operating the free bus service for Brierleys as it approaches the store at the bottom of Belgrave Gate, Leicester. Mike Greenwood

This page, right: **Photographs from the Williams family album showing PUF 647 in service with Southdown outside Horsham station. The lower photos show No 1 newly acquired with Confidence fleet names.** Ken Williams Collection

Below: **Lunchtime break in the Syston Street area of Leicester in 1973 with coach No 2 behind.** Mike Greenwood

Bottom: **PUF 647 returned to original condition as Southdown 547.** Simon Gill

Far left: **LDB 779 in service with North Western as its No 779. It may be about to take up service 28 to Hayfield which was operated by their Manchester depot.** Len Wright

Left: **A rare photo of Confidence No 2 (LDB 779) resting in the Syston Street area in 1973 not long before it was sold.** Mike Greenwood

Below: **LDB 779 is seen in a scrap yard, surrounded by other buses, in August 1975 awaiting its fate.** Stephen Day

AEC Reliance

LDB 779 was one of six similar front line coaches new to North Western Road Car Company, Stockport in March 1959. The under-floor engined AEC Reliance was introduced in 1953 and the 2MU3RA model was fitted with an AEC AH470 7.75 litre engine and air brakes. The body style is often misquoted as 'Contender' but this design was not produced after 1956 being superseded by the 'Wayfarer IV' although, at that time, names were applied very informally by Harrington.

2	LDB 779	AEC Reliance	2MU3RA2357	C41F
		Harrington Wayfarer IV	2065	
	Mar 1959	New to North Western Road Car Co. No 779		
	May 1970	Nesbit Brothers, Somerby, near Melton Mowbray		
	Nov 1971	**Confidence, Oadby, Leicester**		
	Feb 1973	M.V. Patel T/A ABC Coaches, Leicester – withdrawn August 1974		
	Nov 1974	Lancaster, Wootton – withdrawn August 1975		
	Aug 1975	Noted in an unidentified scrap yard		

These coaches were used wherever they were needed but in May 1961 it was allocated to Manchester garage where most of the coaches were based for express services to London, Blackpool, North Wales and across the Pennines.

No 2 entered service with Confidence on 14 November 1971 in Nesbit Bros livery of cream with a blue skirt. After a few months it was repainted mostly grey with a black skirt and, later on, a blue 'CONFIDENCE' fleet name (approx 2ft x 5ins) was applied on the nearside. It was sold to ABC Coaches on 13 February 1973.

After sale, the coach soldiered on for a few years before being noted in a scrap yard in an orange, yellow and black livery with ABC still in the nearside destination indicator. It had been thought that the chassis was exported to Malta but there is no record of this occurring.

Photographs of this coach with Confidence are extremely rare and we have never seen a colour image so, if you can help, please let us know.

Bedford SB

This was the only light-weight bus or coach ever owned and was not considered successful. It was acquired on 15 January 1973 and sold on 15 May 1975.

The Bedford SB was originally introduced at the 1950 Commercial Motor Show and it became a popular coach chassis, especially with smaller operators. It was available with petrol and diesel engines – the SB1 being fitted with a Bedford 4.9 litre diesel engine. The chassis was in continuous production for over 35 years with over 54,000 sold by May 1980, of which 17,482 were for use in the UK.

The Duple Vega body was one of its most successful designs, the 'Super' Vega having a higher standard of interior trim. The '1120' series of body numbers was allocated to the 1960 season when 563 were produced.

Bedford SB1/Duple coach No 3 (456 FUP) is seen parked on Oadby car park on 9 March 1974 with bold, blue CONFIDENCE fleet name. Simon Gill

3	456 FUP	Bedford SB1	75496	C41F
		Duple Super Vega	1120/221	
	Jan 1960	New to GE Martindale, Ferryhill, County Durham becoming Martindale's Coaches Ltd, Ferryhill by July 1964		
	Jul 1966	L.H. Woodley, Felsted, Essex		
	May 1971	County Travel, Leicester and allocated to their Leicester Coach Services fleet in a blue & cream livery, fleet No L3		
	Aug 1971	Transferred to County Travel, repainted in their green & cream livery, fleet No 31		
	Sep 1971	Renumbered 32		
	Jan 1973	Confidence, Oadby, Leicester		
	May 1975	TRS Coach Services, Leicester		
	Oct 1975	Withdrawn by TRS		
	Apr 1976	Ellson & Dowdell (T/A A.M. Coaches), Fleckney, Leics		
	Apr 1978	92nd Leicester Scouts as a Non PSV		
	Unknown	Scrapped		

Right: **One month after being sold, 456 FUP is seen repainted in the grey and red livery of TRS Coaches, Leicester on 28 June 1975. It was parked at Leicester Forest East service station on the M1.** Steve Smith

Far right: **The final owner of 456 FUP was the 92nd Leicester Scouts group. It is seen parked in church grounds at Leicester Forest East on 3 September 1978.** Steve Smith

Leyland Titan PD3

Confidence operated Leyland Titan PD3s for over 20 years. They were ideal buses for school work and served the company well. The PD3 was introduced when the maximum length of a two-axle double deck bus was extended to 30ft; the first examples entering service in 1957. Fitted with a Leyland O.600 9.8 litre diesel engine, the specification of the PD3/4 and PD3A/1 was similar with air brakes and a synchromesh gearbox. The PD3/5 also had air brakes but differed by having a 'Pneumo-cyclic' semi-automatic gearbox. We will look at each one individually.

The forward entrance Northern Counties body was designed specifically for Southdown and was nicknamed 'Queen Mary',

The first ex-Southdown 'Queen Mary' No 4 (XUF 845) is laying over at Syston Street, Leicester on 8 April 1975. Steve Smith

The nearside of 'Queen Mary' Leyland PD3 No 4 (XUF 845) shows how it was ideal for school work – a front entrance with doors rather than an open rear platform which was common in Leicester at the time.
Adrian Rodgers

4	XUF 845	Leyland Titan PD3/4	591977	FH39/30F
		Northern Counties	5414	
	Nov 1959	New to Southdown Motor Services No 845		
	Sep 1971	Transferred to Brighton Hove & District allocation and given SOUTHDOWN-B-H&D fleetname		
	Jul 1973	Sold to Frank Cowley Ltd (dealer), Heywood, Lancashire		
	Aug 1973	**Confidence, Oadby, Leicester**		
	Sep 1980	Sold to Hartwood Exports (Machinery) Ltd (dealer), Birdwell, Barnsley		
	May 1981	West Auckland Grenadiers Junior Jazz Band, West Auckland, Co. Durham for non PSV use. Named 'Annie'		
	Jun 1984	Gone, presumed scrapped		

although how this came about is shrouded in mystery. Between 1958 and 1967 Southdown received 285 of the type with some variations as the design evolved; three of which are represented by those bought by Confidence. Over 100 were exported to Hong Kong when their life on the south coast was over.

Southdown No 845 spent a lot of its life in the Portsmouth area before ending up in Brighton. It was acquired by Confidence on 17 August 1973, collected on 31 August 1973 and withdrawn on 20 September 1980.

9	BUF 272C	Leyland Titan PD3/4	L23974	FH39/30F
		Northern Counties	6194	
	Apr 1965	New to Southdown Motor Services No 272		
	May 1972	Transferred to Brighton Hove & District allocation and given SOUTHDOWN-B-H&D fleetname		
	Jul 1978	**Confidence, Oadby, Leicester**		
	Jul 1993	Seddon, Bushbury for preservation (located at Old Whittington near Chesterfield)		
	Oct 1995	Sold to unknown owner		
	Jul 1996	Firebond Insurance, Cambridge for promotional work		
	Jul 1998	N. Larkin, Alconbury, Cambridgeshire for preservation		
	Sep 2006	Jennings, Ely, Cambridgeshire for continued preservation		
	Sep 2011	D. Mulpeter (Seaford & District), Seaford, East Sussex for continued preservation		
	Jun 2019	Portsmouth City Coaches, Southbourne, West Sussex for continued preservation		

No 9 was the second Southdown 'Queen Mary' PD3 to join the fleet where it ran alongside No 4 for two years. When new it was allocated to Chichester where we believe it stayed until transfer to Brighton, Conway Street garage in May 1972, for use on former Brighton Hove & District routes. This dual fleetname was discontinued in May 1974.

Detail differences to No 4 included twin headlights, a revised moquette seat pattern and three pearlescent panels in the roof to give more light to the upper deck. It was one of the buses that inaugurated the 45 route between the University of Leicester and the Halls of Residence on 6 October 1986.

Confidence sold it for preservation in July 1993 and it was restored into Southdown livery in 1996. Since then it has had several owners and remains active.

Far left: Standing at the entrance to the University of Leicester awaiting its next journey on route 45 to the Halls of Residence at Stoughton Drive South, on 20 October 1986, is No 9 (BUF 272C) the second ex-Southdown Leyland PD3/4 with Northern Counties body. *Simon Gill*

Left: The next day sees No 9 (BUF 272C) at the Halls of Residence on Stoughton Drive South. The red board in the driver's windscreen, stating where the bus is going, is visible in the absence of destination blinds. *Simon Gill*

Above: **Firebond Insurance of Cambridge used BUF 272C for promotional purposes for two years and sponsored a return to its traditional Southdown livery. It is seen at a bus rally during 1997.** *Simon Gill Collection*

Right: **George Jennings and his family then bought BUF 272C for preservation. It is seen at Showbus, Duxford on 27 September 2009.** *Simon Gill*

Far right: **Still in Southdown livery but now sporting 'Seaford & District Motor Services' fleet names in Southdown style script lettering, BUF 272C was at the Kent Showground at Detling on 7 April 2018.** *Simon Gill*

10	PCK 384	Leyland Titan PD3/5		603392	FH41/31F
		Metro-Cammell		Not allocated	
	Jun 1961	New to Ribble Motor Services No 1743			
	Aug 1979	W Norths (PV) Ltd (dealer), Sherburn in Elmet, North Yorkshire			
	Jan 1980	Confidence, Oadby, Leicester			
	Nov 1985	Withdrawn following an accident			
	Jan 1986	Yeates (dealer) for scrap			

After being dissatisfied with the rear-engined Leyland Atlantean, Ribble returned to the PD3 in 1961 with 50 entering service between April and July 1961. With a full-fronted cab they were Ribble's equivalent of the Southdown vehicles although these were bodied by Metro-Cammell of Birmingham and fitted with a 'Pneumo-cyclic' gearbox. The body style was based on MCW's successful 'Orion' design but with deeper skirt panels than usually found on MCW bodies of the period. This is apparent if you compare No 10 to No 11.

It was allocated to Ribble's Carlisle garage when new and stayed there until March 1972 when it moved to Aintree until June 1973. It was next reported at Morecambe in August 1974 where it stayed until withdrawal.

Demonstrating the appearance of what No 10 was like when new is Ribble 1729 (PCK 370) from the same batch of 50 buses. It is now preserved and is shown at a rally in Morecambe on 26 May 2019 to celebrate the centenary of Ribble Motor Services. Simon Gill

No 10 (PCK 384) is shown adjacent to the yard at Spalding Street, where a start has been made to apply red lining below the back two lower deck windows to separate the black and grey livery. John Bennett

The advertising hoardings on Humberstone Road are shown to good effect as No 10 (PCK 384) passes Pembroke Street Post Office on a sunny winter's day. The red lining out on the livery is now in evidence. Mike Greenwood

No 10 initially entered service with Confidence in Ribble livery before being repainted. It was fitted with a centrifugal clutch and was very noisy. Unfortunately, on Tuesday 5 November 1985 on its way to Longslade School, Birstall it suffered a head-on crash with a Mercedes lorry that was travelling too fast. Luckily, the driver, Ken Williams was able to anticipate what was going to happen and jumped onto the bonnet avoiding serious injury – the driver's side taking the full impact. The damage was too severe to repair so the bus was withdrawn.

11	GRY 55D	Leyland Titan PD3A/1	L60644	H41/33RD
	Metro-Cammell		Not allocated	
	Jun 1966	New to Leicester City Transport No 55		
	May 1980	Withdrawn by Leicester City Transport		
	Jul 1980	Confidence, Oadby, Leicester		
	Aug 1980	Platform doors fitted by Astill & Jordan, Ratby, Leicester		
	Jul 1994	Seddon & Milson (Peakbus), Bushbury (see below)		
	Unknown	Alder, Clacton for preservation		
	Aug 2000	'Viking Pub' St. Fleur, France		
	Unknown	Sold for conversion into a mobile home but later vandalised		

No 11 was the only PD3 in the fleet with a rear entrance. It entered service with Leicester City Transport on 4 June 1966 fitted with an 'Orion' style rear entrance body with an open platform. It was sold to Confidence in July 1980 for £765 including tyres plus VAT.

On acquisition, the open platform was not considered suitable for use on school contracts so, in August 1980, four leaf air operated doors were fitted by Mick Gamble of Astill & Jordan at their Ratby premises. The doors came from an ex-London Transport DMS Daimler Fleetline that was being broken up at Wombwell Diesels, Barnsley. The opportunity was also taken to repaint No 11 in Confidence livery, being the first one to gain red lining between the grey and black colours.

In March 1990, No 11 was lent to Nottingham City Transport for driver training. NCT supplied Leyland Atlantean/East Lancs No 599 (GVO 719N) to Confidence in exchange until June 1990 when No 11 returned.

Despite its rear platform it lasted in service until 10 July 1994 when it was the last PD3 in the fleet to be withdrawn. It was sold to new operator, Seddon & Milson T/A 'Peakbus' of Bushbury, for their services based at Old Whittington, near Chesterfield. It entered service on 12 July working services 29 & 458 and subsequently ran as a free bus ahead of Chesterfield Transport services 20, 54 & 43. Peakbus ceased trading in March 1996. It is likely Alder, Clacton acquired it for preservation around that time. We believe it was then sold to Carl Ireland (dealer), Hull who exported it to the Viking Pub at St Fleur, France. It was last reported vandalised and its current status is unknown.

No 12 was one of the final four 'Queen Marys' to enter service with Southdown in July 1967 (along with Nos 350, 351 & 354). Unlike Nos 4 & 9, the Northern Counties body has distinctive panoramic windows and a curved upper deck windscreen. It was allocated to Worthing in November 1970 and by February 1979, Brighton, although it did not form part of the former BH&D network. It was

Top left: **Leicester City Transport No 55 (GRY 55D) is seen in Humberstone Gate, Leicester departing on route 20 to Imperial Avenue when fairly new in 1966.** Peter Newland Collection

Top right: **Leicester City Transport dispensed with the top crimson band during 1968 and No 55 was repainted as shown on 31 October 1970. It was also fitted with lower case destination blinds and is seen in Charles Street heading for Eyres Monsell on route 88.** Peter Newland Collection

Centre: **With all the other PD3s having a full front, the half-cab nature of No 11 is shown to good effect in this view at Bagworth on 5 June 1993.** Simon Gill

Bottom: **The neat conversion to rear platform doors, together with an emergency exit in the back panel, is shown to good effect in this view.** Simon Gill

12	HCD 356E	Leyland Titan PD3/4	L64215	FH39/30F
		Northern Counties	6482	
	Jun 1967	New to Southdown Motor Services No 356		
	Mar 1980	Withdrawn by Southdown and placed in store		
	Jan 1981	Confidence, Oadby, Leicester		
	Aug 1991	L. Strangman, Gawcott, Buckinghamshire		
	Aug 2014	C. Pearce, Worthing for preservation		
	Jul 2015	D. Mulpeter, Seaford, East Sussex for continued preservation		
	Jun 2017	C. Pearce, Worthing for continued preservation		

one of the last Panoramics to be withdrawn in March 1980 when it was placed in store.

Acquired by Confidence in January 1981 as No 12 it initially ran in Southdown NBC livery before being repainted black and grey during the Easter school holiday. It was a very reliable bus but water ingress from the panoramic windows was a constant problem.

After withdrawal in August 1991 it was sold to Laurie Strangman of Gawcott, Buckinghamshire for use as a commentary box at various equestrian events and polo matches. It has since been bought for preservation.

When Leyland PD3 No 12 (HCD 356E) arrived it was initially used in Southdown NBC livery of green with a white band. It is seen in Humberstone Gate on 31 March 1981 shortly before repainting during the Easter holiday. Steve Smith

As noted earlier, No 12 was the second bus to be used on the inaugural day of service 45 on 6 October 1986. It is seen leaving the University of Leicester at the end of its first journey. The red destination board on the front stands out clearly. Simon Gill

Photographed at the Southdown Centenary Rally at Southsea Common on 7 June 2015, No 12 displays signs of its previous green livery. Simon Gill

Leyland Leopard L2

The first of ten Leyland Leopards to enter the Confidence fleet, No 5 was originally one of five delivered to Southdown in October 1963 (Nos 1749-1753) built to the 'Grenadier' design with panoramic windows but with a 'Cavalier' front panel under the windscreen. The body was 31ft 10ins long on a 30ft chassis and originally seated C28F with 2 + 1 seating, as a front line UK touring coach. It also featured air suspension and forced air ventilation. The entire batch was stored until the beginning of the 1964 season. It was downgraded from touring after the 1971 season and refurbished by ECW to C39F using low backed green vinyl seats without headrests. 749 DCD was subsequently withdrawn in early 1975.

Acquired by Confidence and noted on 9 March 1975 in Oadby still in Southdown livery, it was repainted in fleet livery of grey with a black skirt during the Easter school holiday and given fleet No 5. It is the only Confidence vehicle that has ever been used on an overseas trip when it travelled to Paris. In March 1977 it was hit by a Midland Red Leyland National at the top of Nursery Road, Leicester which damaged the air suspension. It was repaired by Yeates of Loughborough.

On 21 December 1985 a group of Leicester enthusiasts, including the authors, used No 5 for a farewell tour around the Bradgate Park and Charnwood Forest areas of Leicestershire. It was sold to David Dean of Paisley as part of his 'Classique' fleet but, as far as we know, was never used.

The third coach to be acquired by Confidence to replace Bedford No 3, was No 5 (749 DCD) the popular Leyland Leopard L2 with Harrington 'Grenadier' coachwork. The design incorporated a 'Cavalier' front panel as Southdown wanted to standardise on this to make accident damage repair easier. It is parked at Spalding Street depot. Trevor Follows

The farewell tour on 21 December 1985 saw No 5 tour the Bradgate and Charnwood Forest areas of Leicestershire. Simon Gill

Restored to its former glory as Southdown front line touring coach No 1749 complete with armchair seats, 749 DCD was one of the stars at the Southdown Centenary Rally at Southsea Common on 7 June 2015. Simon Gill

Fortunately, 749 DCD was purchased for ongoing preservation by Graham Burtenshaw, Chichester in March 1999. He has done a very thorough restoration to original Southdown condition complete with those sumptuous reclining armchair seats. It now forms part of his associated Southcoast Motor Services Ltd heritage fleet where it is available for hire.

5	749 DCD	Leyland Leopard L2		L02114	C39F
		Harrington Grenadier		2840	
	Oct 1963	Delivered to Southdown Motor Services No 1749			
	May 1964	Placed in service			
	Dec 1971	Interior renovation by Eastern Coach Works (ECW), Lowestoft and re-seated to C39F – Job no R1148			
	Feb 1972	Returned to service with Southdown			
	Feb 1975	Sold to Frank Cowley Ltd (dealer), Heywood, Lancashire			
	Mar 1975	Confidence, Oadby, Leicester			
	Jan 1986	Dean (T/A Classique Sun Saloon Luxury Coaches), Paisley for preservation and placed in store			
	Mar 1999	G Burtenshaw, Chichester for preservation			
	Mar 2007	Restored to C28F			
	Nov 2013	South Coast Motor Services, Croydon for continued preservation			

Bristol Lodekkas

The Bristol Lodekka with Eastern Coach Works (ECW) body was built exclusively for the nationalised British Transport Commission fleets that acquired the Tilling Group's bus interests in September 1948, including these two manufacturers. The Lodekka was a revolutionary design. By splitting the transmission into two, thereby providing a propeller shaft to each pair of rear wheels, it enabled a low floor with central gangways on both decks but within a low overall height of 13ft 4ins. Initially seating 58 passengers, the interior was altered from 1955 to enable 60 people to be accommodated sitting down.

Both examples acquired by Confidence featured the chassis manufacturer's own Bristol AVW 8.25 litre engine, together with a constant mesh gearbox and vacuum brakes. A total of 2,179 were built before the model was superseded by the 'F' series in late 1959.

Above: **LRU 72 when almost new as Hants & Dorset No 1342 on route 38 to Bournemouth. It is still fitted with its original 'long apron' radiator grille and deep front wings which were later shortened to improve air flow to the front brakes.** Peter Yeomans

6	LRU 72	Bristol Lodekka LD6B	100.063		H33/25RD
		Eastern Coach Works	6621		
	Jun 1954	New to Hants & Dorset Motor Services, Bournemouth No 1342			
	Sep 1971	Re-numbered 1406			
	Sep 1975	W Norths (PV) Ltd (dealer), Sherburn in Elmet, North Yorkshire			
	Nov 1975	Confidence, Oadby, Leicester			
	Nov 1976	Dismantled for spares and remains scrapped			

New to Hants & Dorset in June 1954 it entered service on 1 July. As with all early Bristol Lodekkas it had a 'long apron' radiator grille and long front wings. During 1956/7 the front wings were shortened to improve air flow to the front brakes and a shorter radiator grille was fitted in 1956. Under seat heaters were fitted in October 1959, together with flashing direction indicators about the same time. We believe it spent most of its life in the Bournemouth area before being withdrawn after the 1975 summer season.

It was sold to the well know dealer, Norths of Sherburn in Elmet, North Yorkshire around September 1975 and acquired by Confidence on 4 November 1975. It was repainted in the black and grey livery in stages during December 1975 and completed by Christmas.

Above: **No 6 fully repainted and parked by the entrance to Oadby car park in early 1976 with No 4 (XUF 845) behind. A cover on the front grille ensures the radiator does not get too cold during the winter months.** Simon Gill

Below: **A few months later on 8 April 1976 No 6 is seen, once again with No 4 behind, parked at Syston Street, Leicester awaiting its next trip.** Steve Smith

It was the oldest bus ever owned but worked hard and performed well; a tribute to the quality of the chassis and body manufacturers. It was withdrawn and scrapped by Confidence in November 1976 after removal of useful mechanical and body parts.

Left: **Not long after arriving in Oadby in 1975, No 6 (LRU 72) is seen with some lower panels repainted in black and grey. The upper deck remains in Hants & Dorset livery. Note the shorter radiator grille and front wings.** Simon Gill

A similar type of bus to No 6, this was new to Southern National on 1 March 1957 and transferred to Western National on 25 November 1969 when the two companies merged. We believe it mostly operated from Yeovil garage in Somerset.

Initially delicensed after the 1975 summer season it was placed in store but, due to the late delivery of replacement Bristol VRTs, it was overhauled, repainted and re-certified in early 1976, gaining a new four year Certificate of Fitness (CoF). In the meantime, the new buses arrived and, judging by tickets found on the bus, it is believed it only ran for a day or two before withdrawal so was acquired in superb condition.

Again, it gave excellent service to Confidence and was only withdrawn when its CoF expired on 31 January 1980.

7	UOD 500	Bristol Lodekka LD6B	130.135		H33/27RD
	Eastern Coach Works		9187		
Mar 1957	New to Southern National Omnibus Company, Exeter No 1917				
Nov 1969	Transferred to Western National with the rest of the Southern National business retaining No 1917				
May 1976	W Norths (PV) Ltd (dealer), Sherburn in Elmet, North Yorkshire				
Nov 1976	Confidence, Oadby, Leicester				
Feb 1980	G. Jones (Carlton Metals), (dealer), Carlton, Barnsley for scrap				

Below: **Bristol Lodekka with ECW body, UOD 500 as Southern National 1917, at Taunton Bus Station awaiting its next trip on route 264 back to Yeovil.** Peter Legg Collection

Right: **Parked in Yeovil bus station around 1973 is Western National 1917 (UOD 500). It retains Tilling green and cream livery but has bold Western National fleet names in NBC style lettering.**
Colin Billington Collection

Far right: **No 7 (UOD 500) is seen in the yard behind the Queen Victoria pub at High Street, Syston on 6 May 1979 following the move from Oadby to the other side of the county.**
Steve Smith

Leyland Leopard PSU3 Bus

Far left: Newly acquired No 8 (273 AUF) is seen on Oadby car park on 28 March 1977. It is a Leyland Leopard PSU3/1R with Marshall 49-seat body that came from East Kent and initially retained NBC poppy red livery. It was originally new to Southdown. Simon Gill

Left: No 8 was repainted into Confidence coach livery of grey with a black skirt. It retained the red beading below the windows which looked attractive; preceding the introduction of red lining on double-deckers by three years. It is seen at the High Street, Syston yard on 29 August 1977. Steve Smith

When the maximum length of single deck buses was increased to 36ft (11m) in 1961 this was one of the first buses acquired by Southdown to the newly extended dimension. The PSU3/1R was fitted with a synchromesh gearbox and the Marshall body was built to the standard BET Federation design. When new it was fitted with 51 bus seats for operation by a crew and allocated to Portsmouth where we believe it remained throughout its time with Southdown.

In December 1965 it was down-seated to B45F, with luggage pens either side at the front of the saloon, and fitted for one-person-operation. East Kent bought it in November 1971 to extend one-person-operation in Folkestone and fitted two extra pairs of seats, supplied by Southdown, in December. It entered service in February 1972 after repainting in traditional East Kent livery. It was repainted into NBC poppy red livery in June 1975 when it also received refurbished seats in East Kent moquette.

It is the only single deck bus Confidence has operated, being acquired hastily on 24 March 1977 to cover for Leopard coach No 5 after it was damaged in an accident. It entered service in East Kent livery before being repainted grey with a black skirt. It was only operated for a year, being sold on 29 May 1978 to local operator, Straws of Leicester where it became the last vehicle purchased by that concern before the firm closed in March 1979. It went on to see service with two other operators until sale for preservation in June 1996. It is now back in a version of the livery it carried with East Kent.

8	273 AUF	Leyland Leopard PSU3/1R	623838	B49F
		Marshall	**B3116**	
	Mar 1963	New to Southdown Motor Services, Brighton, No 673 as B51F		
	Dec 1965	Re-seated to B45F for one-person-operation		
	Nov 1971	Sold to East Kent Road Car Company, Canterbury		
	Dec 1971	Re-seated to B49F		
	Feb 1977	Ensign (dealer), Hornchurch, Kent		
	Mar 1977	**Confidence, Oadby, Leicester**		
	May 1978	Straws of Leicester Ltd, Leicester		
	Apr 1979	Galloway European Coachlines, Mendlesham, Suffolk		
	Aug 1981	Rule's Coaches, Boxford, Suffolk – withdrawn June 1993		
	Jun 1996	J. Cooper, Newcastle-under-Lyme, Staffordshire for preservation, relocating to Shadoxhurst, Kent in March 2001		
	Sep 2008	J. Cooper, Shadoxhurst, Kent, P. Drake, Deal, Kent & D. Ferguson, Ramsgate, Kent for continued preservation		

Above: After operation by Rules of Boxford, 273 AUF was sold for preservation. Restoration was under way when it was seen in the grounds of Dover Transport Museum on 12 August 2017. Simon Gill Collection

Left: External restoration had been completed with a repaint into a version of East Kent livery by 7 April 2018. It is seen at the Detling Rally at Kent Showground that day. Simon Gill

Leyland Leopard PSU Coaches

The Leyland Leopard PSU range was a common and very popular chassis for 20 years until superseded by the Tiger in 1982. The PSU3 was 36ft (11m) long and the PSU4 was the shorter 30ft 10ins (9.4m) model. The specification was improved in 1968 with a suffix letter 'A' added to the type code when the Leyland O.680 11.1 litre engine was offered. This continued on all subsequent models and was fitted to all the coaches below. A further change in 1971 introduced the 'B' version with new, upgraded axles. The 'E' range introduced from 1978 had improved brakes, gearbox and relocated aid reservoirs, the 'F', in 1979, having another revised gearbox, before the final 'G' model from 1981 featured a rationalised engine. All the coaches operated by Confidence were fitted with the Pneumo-cyclic gearbox.

13	AHA 451J	Leyland Leopard PSU4B/4R	7101365	C40F
		Plaxton Panorama Elite II	713057	
	May 1971	New to Birmingham & Midland Motor Omnibus Company (Midland Red) No 6451		
	Sep 1981	Midland Red (Express) No 6451		
	Jan 1982	Midland Red (East) No 6451		
	Oct 1982	Stored before withdrawal in May 1983		
	Aug 1983	Confidence, Leicester		
	Jun 1997	R. White, Leicester for preservation		
	Jan 2004	Birmingham & Midland Motor Omnibus Trust for continued preservation		
	Mar 2004	D. Potts, Birmingham for continued preservation		

New to Midland Red as a front line touring coach in their traditional red livery, it was allocated to Bearwood garage for the first season before moving to Leicester, Southgate Street in May 1972. Most touring coaches were delicensed and stored during the winter months and, in November 1972, it received NBC 'National' all over white livery. It then moved around the Leicester garages until April 1976 when it spent two years at Tamworth. Initially withdrawn in January 1978 it was reinstated at Leicester, Sandacre Street in May 1979 before a move to Digbeth, Birmingham in May 1980. It then moved to Wigston in April 1981 where it remained throughout the split up of Midland Red, until sale to Confidence where it gained an overall grey livery.

Purchased for preservation, it has been restored into Midland Red 'National' white coach livery and can be seen at the Transport Museum, Wythall.

14	AHA 452J	Leyland Leopard PSU4B/4R	7101122	C40F
		Plaxton Panorama Elite II	713058	
	May 1971	New to Birmingham & Midland Motor Omnibus Company (Midland Red) No 6452		
	Sep 1981	Midland Red (Express) No 6452		
	Jan 1982	Midland Red (East) No 6452		
	Jan 1984	Midland Red (East) renamed Midland Fox		
	May 1985	Withdrawn and stored		
	Dec 1985	Confidence, Leicester		
	Aug 1994	Scrapped		

Like No 13 this coach was new to Midland Red as a front line touring coach in traditional red livery allocated to Bearwood garage for the first season before moving to Leicester, Southgate Street in May 1972. It was repainted in NBC 'National' all over white livery in January 1973. Delicensed and stored during the winter months it remained mostly at Southgate Street until initial withdrawal in January 1978. Reinstated at Leicester, Sandacre Street in May 1979 it also moved to Digbeth, Birmingham in May 1980 where it remained when Midland Red was split up. On transfer to Midland Red (East) in January 1982 it moved to Wigston garage until withdrawal and sale to Confidence where it gained an overall grey livery.

Below left: **When new to Midland Red these two coaches carried this all over red livery which looked very smart with bright aluminium trim. Midland Red 6452 (AHA 452J) is seen during a Scottish tour when brand new on 2 June 1971.** The late Derek Bailey/Trevor Follows Collection

Below: **Confidence No 13 (AHA 451J) is laying over at Humberstone Gate, Leicester on 6 February 1989. Although the weather is dry it has clearly been wet given the dirt behind the wheels on the side panels.** Simon Gill

Since being sold for preservation No 13 has been restored in National White coach livery with Midland Red fleet names. It is seen during an open day at the Transport Museum, Wythall on 10 October 2004.
Simon Gill

In May 1984, after Midland Red East had changed its name to Midland Fox, No 6452 is seen in the yard at Southgate Street depot with National Express red and blue stripes added to the all-over white livery.
Trevor Follows

On 12 September 1992 Confidence No 14 (AHA 452J) awaits its passengers in all-over grey livery. Trevor Follows

31	XRR 616M	Leyland Leopard PSU3B/4R	7300600		C53F
		Plaxton Elite Express III	733753		
	Aug 1973	New to Barton Transport, Chilwell, Notts No 1287			
	Jul 1989	Wellglade Group takeover of Barton Transport No 1287			
	Aug 1994	**Confidence, Leicester**			
	Jan 2002	Scrapped at the depot			

The Leyland Leopard/Plaxton coach with folding entrance doors was a popular combination with Barton as they could be used on express as well as local stage carriage services. Barton operated throughout Nottinghamshire, Derbyshire, Leicestershire and Rutland, together with neighbouring counties which included a depot in Highcross Street, Leicester. Barton Transport sold its coach, bus and travel business, including its fleet and stock, to the Wellglade Group on 2 July 1989 where it was eventually merged with Trent.

It received the overall grey livery at Confidence and was regularly used on the Sunday stage carriage services.

32	UVO 125S	Leyland Leopard PSU3E/4R	7703713		C49F
		Duple Dominant Express	734/5331		
	Nov 1977	New to Trent Motor Traction Company, Derby No 125			
	Apr 1989	Loaned to Barton Transport 29 April 1989 until 1 July 1989			
	Aug 1990	Repainted into Barton Buses livery and renumbered No 1125			
	May 1994	Withdrawn			
	Aug 1994	**Confidence, Leicester**			
	Jul 1996	Loaned to Worths Motor Services, Enstone, Oxfordshire until January 1997			
	Oct 1998	Scrapped after accident			

No 32 was one of eight similar coaches new to Trent in November 1977 painted in the NBC dual purpose livery of poppy red and white. In July 1982 it was allocated to Matlock garage where it remained for several years. As noted above, it was loaned to Barton Transport from April 1989 until the takeover by Wellglade on 2 July 1989 where it remained with Barton, which was then a Group subsidiary like Trent, until 21 July 1989 when it returned to Trent. In August 1990 it was repainted in Barton livery, operating on loan until the move was made permanent in August 1993 until withdrawal.

On acquisition by Confidence it received the all over grey livery. It was a regular performer on their Sunday evening Leicester City Council contracts on routes 21, 22 and 39. An accident in October 1998 led to its early withdrawal.

Parked receiving attention at Spalding Street depot is No 31 (XRR 616M) in the all-over grey coach livery. Trevor Follows

Confidence No 31 (XRR 616M) is shown on Leicester's Outer Ring road whilst on a school trip. Adrian Rodgers

Confidence No 32 (UVO 132S) was the only Duple Dominant coach operated and looked very smart standing in the summer sunshine, the black front grille contrasting well with the light grey livery. An accident led to its early withdrawal. Adrian Rodgers

Left: Shortly after sale for preservation No 34 retained its later red and black Confidence livery but with fleet names and fleet numbers removed. It is shown at Chatsworth House, Derbyshire on 25 June 2006 with lower front fog lamps reinstated. *Simon Gill*

Below left: By 28 September 2008 No 34 had been restored to its original Barton livery as No 564. It was on display at Showbus, Duxford. *Simon Gill*

Below: When they are no longer required many buses and coaches have been dismantled over the years to provide spare parts for similar vehicles still in service. This view demonstrates the thorough job that is done by Confidence staff as No 35 is in the closing stages of being cannibalised on 7 June 2003. *Simon Gill*

Below: Repainted into red and black livery, No 36 awaits departure on an enthusiasts' excursion on 11 August 2007. It was sold three months later. *Simon Gill*

34	KAU 564V	Leyland Leopard PSU3E/4R	7930029	C53F
		Plaxton Supreme IV Express	8011LX539	
	Jul 1980	New to Barton Transport, Chilwell, Notts No 564		
	Jul 1989	Wellglade Group takeover of Barton Transport, renumbered No 1564		
	Mar 1996	**Confidence, Leicester**		
	Apr 2006	Notts & Derby Heritage Transport Group, Ravenshead, Notts for preservation		
	Oct 2006	Towle & Campbell, Awsworth, Notts for continued preservation		
	Jul 2013	Rogan, Ripley, Derbyshire for continued preservation		
	Mar 2018	Nottingham Heritage Vehicles, Hucknall for continued preservation		

No 34 is the updated version of No 31 with improved chassis and the later Plaxton Supreme IV Express body. A detail difference between this, similar No 35 and the two later Leopards, is the thin bright trim below the side windows which was omitted on Nos 36 & 37. The history of No 34 prior to arrival at Confidence is similar to No 31. After initially carrying the all-over grey Confidence livery, it received the new red and black coach livery.

Upon withdrawal, it was saved for preservation where it has passed through several owners. It is now restored in original Barton livery as No 564 and is part of the Nottingham Heritage Vehicles collection based at the former Trent depot at Hucknall, Nottingham.

35	LNU 569W	Leyland Leopard PSU3E/4R	7930017	C53F
		Plaxton Supreme IV Express	8011LX547	
	Sep 1980	New to Barton Transport, Chilwell, Notts No 569		
	July 1989	Wellglade Group takeover of Barton Transport, renumbered No 1569		
	Mar 1996	**Confidence, Leicester**		
	June 2003	Dismantled for spares and remains scrapped at depot		

Purchased from Trent Barton Buses at the same time as No 34, it has a similar history to its stable mate. It did not last as long and was dismantled at the depot on withdrawal.

36	VRC 611Y	Leyland Leopard PSU3G/4R	8231066	C53F
		Plaxton Supreme V Express	8211LLS5X514	
	Sep 1982	New to Barton Transport, Chilwell, Notts No 611		
	Jul 1989	Wellglade Group takeover of Barton Transport, renumbered No 1611		
	Nov 1996	**Confidence, Leicester**		
	Nov 2007	Nottingham Heritage Vehicles, Mansfield, Notts for preservation		
	May 2010	Looms (dealer), Spondon, Derbyshire for scrap		

This coach was significant as being the penultimate of the last ten Plaxton-bodied Leyland Leopards to be built. As well as having the final version of the Leopard chassis, it was fitted with the final Supreme V Express body which was similar to the IV except for a redesigned rear with a shallower window, deeper illuminated display panel and larger rear light clusters.

Whilst in service with Barton it was used from Nottingham garage; being withdrawn in July 1996. Briefly reinstated by Trent it was withdrawn in October 1996. After starting in all-over grey livery it later received the red and black scheme. It was sold for preservation to Nottingham Heritage Vehicles and rallied in Confidence livery. Sadly it did not survive and was scrapped in May 2010.

The distinctive rear of the Plaxton Supreme V Express body on No 36, which only appeared on this final batch of Barton coaches, shows the shallower rear window and revised light clusters. The deeper illuminated display glass below the window has been painted over. Simon Gill

37	PTV 591X	Leyland Leopard PSU3F/4R	8130830	C53F
		Plaxton Supreme IV Express	8111LX576	
	Sep 1981	New to Barton Transport, Chilwell, Notts No 591		
	Jul 1989	Wellglade Group takeover of Barton Transport, renumbered No 1591		
	Aug 1996	Cygnet, Darton, South Yorkshire No 19		
	Sep 1997	**Confidence, Leicester**		
	Mar 2007	Nottingham Heritage Vehicles, Mansfield, Notts for preservation		
	Jun 2010	Scrapped by this date		

Once again, No 37 had a similar history to the other former Barton coaches. It was allocated to their main depot at Chilwell from new until February 1994 when it moved to Nottingham. Withdrawn by Barton Buses in June 1996 it passed to Cygnet, Darton for a year before acquisition by Confidence. After being repainted in all-over grey livery it later received the red and black scheme. It was also sold for preservation to Nottingham Heritage Vehicles but did not survive and was scrapped by June 2010.

The last Leyland Leopard to be bought by Confidence was No 37 (PTV 591X). It was at the Wigston depot on 7 June 2003. Simon Gill

AEC Routemasters

15	WLT 655	AEC Routemaster		R2RH651		H36/28R
		Park Royal		L5161		
	Jan 1961	New to London Transport No RM655, stored at Loughton garage				
	Apr 1961	Into service from Wood Green garage on 127, 259 & 269 routes				
	Jun 1965	Overhaul – body no B621				
	Jul 1972	Overhaul – body no B606 and transferred to Edmonton garage				
	Mar 1974	Transferred to Enfield garage				
	May 1975	Repainted at Aldenham works and returned to Enfield				
	Apr 1977	Overhaul – body no B96 and transferred to Sidcup garage				
	Feb 1980	Repainted at Aldenham works and returned to Sidcup				
	Nov 1981	Overhaul – body no B1883, fitted with a Leyland engine and transferred to West Ham garage				
	Jul 1984	Withdrawn and placed in store at Turnham Green then AEC Southall				
	Aug 1985	**Confidence, Oadby, Leicester**				
	Nov 1985	Into service with Confidence				

Nearly everyone knows the name Routemaster – the iconic red London bus. Designed by London Transport with AEC and Park Royal, it was very advanced when the first one emerged in 1954 with features such as integral construction with two sub-frames, an aluminium alloy body, independent front suspension, hydraulic brakes, AEC direct selection/automatic gearbox and power assisted steering.

After extensive testing of four prototypes, production commenced in 1959 and 2,875 were built over the next nine years. Most were fitted with AEC engines but both those with Confidence had Leyland O.600 9.8 litre engines. The extensive overhaul programme used by London Transport saw bodies swapped each time a bus was overhauled. This is reflected in the history of the two Routemasters.

The final body (B1883) fitted to No 15 was new in April 1964. We believe it was one of the first Routemasters sold direct by LT to a private operator. LT cleaned and silvered the underneath, fitted new tyres and tested it before sale.

It was initially placed in storage at Emblings, Guyhirn, Cambridgeshire but was collected on Wednesday 6 November 1985, entering service the following day in LT red livery, to replace accident damaged PD3 No 10 (PCK 384) on a Gartree High School, Oadby school contract.

On the first day of stage carriage operation on Monday 6 October 1986 on Route 45, No 15 was the first arrival at the University of Leicester from the Halls of Residence at 9.15am. It then saw regular use on the 45 until the service ceased. Regular use on school and works contracts followed until 2003, since when it has been largely confined to private hire for weddings and funerals. It attended the RM40 and RM50 celebrations in London to mark these significant milestones of the popular Routemaster.

After 34 years in service with Confidence, No 15 must be a contender for the longest serving Routemaster with a second operator.

Above: **In service with London Transport on route 5 to Waterloo is RM655 bearing the later white LT 'roundel' on the side.** Paul Redmond

Left: **Oyez! Oyez! In November 1997 Confidence No 15 (WLT 655) was used to promote a 12-hour shopping spectacular at Debenhams department store. It is seen parked in Humberstone Gate with the Town Crier encouraging visitors with his familiar call.** Tom Moore

Opposite, top: **All ready for its next wedding with a lucky horseshoe on the radiator grille, No 15 was at a bus rally at Quorn & Woodhouse railway station on 26 April 2013.** Simon Gill

Bottom left: **A rear view of smart looking No 15 during a refreshment break on its way to attend the RM50 celebration at Finsbury Park on 24 July 2004.** Simon Gill

Upper and lower right: **The smart upper deck on No 15 and the lower deck, below, remain in LT condition including an advert on the front bulkhead of the lower saloon.** Simon Gill

17	WLT 621	AEC Routemaster	R2RH617	H36/28R
		Park Royal	L5199	
	Jan 1961	New to London Transport No RM621, stored at Loughton garage		
	Apr 1961	Into service from Wood Green garage on 127, 259 & 269 routes		
	May 1965	Overhaul – body no B605		
	Feb 1970	Transferred to Walthamstow garage		
	May 1972	Overhaul – body no B580 and transferred to Abbey Wood garage		
	Apr 1975	Repainted at Aldenham works and returned to Abbey Wood		
	Apr 1977	Overhaul – body no B520 and transferred to Willesden garage		
	Oct 1977	Transferred to Wood Green garage		
	Jul 1978	Transferred to Harrow Weald garage for the 140 route		
	Apr 1980	Repainted at Aldenham works and returned to Harrow Weald		
	Oct 1981	Transferred to Aldenham as a Works Float		
	Feb 1982	Overhaul – body no B1920, fitted with a Leyland engine and transferred to Streatham		
	Oct 1984	Transferred to Norwood garage		
	Oct 1985	Withdrawn and placed in store at Turnham Green then AEC Southall		
	May 1986	**Confidence, Oadby, Leicester**		
	Oct 1990	Withdrawn after an accident on 28 September 1990 and taken to Brierley Hill Salvage (dealer), Brierley Hill, West Midlands		
	Oct 1990	Brown (Shaftsbury & District), Motcombe, Dorset for preservation		
	Apr 1992	Rebuilt by Brown (Shaftsbury & District) and fitted with an AEC engine		
	May 1993	On loan to BHT Buses Ltd T/A Routemaster Bournemouth, Bournemouth from Brown T/A Vale of Blackmore Travel, Motcombe and repainted in Routemaster Bournemouth livery No 281 until February 1994		
	Aug 1994	Greater Reading Omnibus Co (T/A Reading Mainline), Reading		
	Oct 1994	Into service with Reading Mainline No 16		
	May 1998	Reading Mainline acquired by Reading Transport, retained No 16		
	Aug 1998	Exported to Argentina		

In addition to the history shown, RM621 was stored for short periods between December 1974 and March 1976 during its time at Abbey Wood garage. Its final body (B1920) was new in May 1964.

No 17 was acquired by Confidence on 26 May 1986 and initially used in LT red until it was repainted during the school summer holiday. Unfortunately, its stay was curtailed when it was involved in a serious accident on Friday 28 September 1990 at the junction of Green Lane Road and East Park Road which caused it to collide with a shop front. When the Confidence team went to collect No 17 it had already been towed away so they never saw it again. It was repaired, used by several operators and is now in Argentina.

Top left: **In LT livery with grey between decks band and gold underlined London Transport fleet name is RM 621 (WLT 621) on route 221 to Finsbury Park Station.** Paul Redmond

Top right: **A slight change in livery sees a white band and bulls eye roundel on RM621 as it heads to West Hampstead on route 159.** Paul Redmond

Above: **Confidence No 17 (WLT 621) has just turned off Victoria Park Road into Queens Road on Sunday 24 June 1990 whilst operating the 10, Inner Link service to Narborough Road.** Simon Gill

Below left: **After the repair of accident damage, WLT 621 operated for Routemaster Bournemouth as No 281 in competition with the council owned Bournemouth Transport. It is seen at Bournemouth Square in 1993.** Adrian Rodgers

Below: **Repainted in Reading Mainline livery, WLT 621 operated as No 16 until export to Argentina in 1998.** Adrian Rodgers

Leyland Atlantean/Alexander

The Leyland Atlantean was introduced in 1958 as a 30ft long rear-engined chassis. Early examples were not the most reliable due to lack of testing and drivers no longer being able to hear the engine so were unable to refine their driving technique. The longer 33ft (10m) PDR2/1 model with a larger Leyland O.680 11.1 litre engine and updated version of the SCG Pneumo-cyclic gearbox was introduced in 1968. Production of the PDR series models ended when they were replaced by the AN68 in 1972.

Although fitted with the same O.680 engine the AN68 was much improved, robust and reliable selling in large numbers to UK and overseas buyers. The AN68/1R was 30ft 10ins (9.4m) long and the AN68A/1R incorporated an electronic automated control system. Confidence found the AN68 to be the ideal replacement for the front engined double deckers and to expand the fleet.

16	WTN 640H	Leyland Atlantean PDR2/1	901700	H48/30D
		Alexander	J15/568/9	
	Dec 1969	New to Newcastle Corporation No 640		
	Jan 1970	Tyneside PTE No 640		
	Apr 1974	Tyne & Wear PTE No 640		
	Jan 1981	Rennie, Dunfermline, Fife		
	Jun 1982	Lloyd, Nuneaton, Warwickshire		
	Dec 1985	**Confidence, Leicester**		
	Dec 1988	Withdrawn and used as a shield and seat store at Wigston depot		
	Dec 2000	Scrapped		

No 16 was, numerically, Newcastle Corporation's last new vehicle prior to transfer to Tyneside PTE on 1 January 1970 which later became Tyne & Wear PTE on 1 April 1974. It was unusual in being a 33ft long example, PDR2/1; with Alexander J-type body featuring dual doors, a nearside staircase and panoramic windows.

It was the first rear-engined bus in the Confidence fleet and was purchased as a permanent replacement for the accident damaged Leyland Titan PD3 No 10 (PCK 384). Nicknamed 'The Beast', as it was never popular with drivers, the centre doors were sealed and it entered service in Lloyds livery, being repainted black and grey during the summer of 1986. It was fitted for one person operation in September 1986 for use on the stage service if required.

Its withdrawal was hastened following a rear end collision in Aikman Avenue, Leicester, when it was hit by Midland Fox MCW Metroliner double deck coach No 7052 (C52 VJU). Repairing the damage to get it through its next MOT was not justified.

After withdrawal, it was used for storage and to shield other members of the fleet from attacks by vandals at the Harrison Close, South Wigston depot, whilst newly planted conifers grew. It continued in this role until 24 November 2000 when it was replaced by Atlantean No 27. Its remains were towed to a nearby scrap dealer early the following month.

Top: **WTN 640H is seen in Gallowgate, Newcastle, operating the 'Rail Link' service R4 as Tyneside PTE No 640.** Simon Gill Collection

Above: **No 16 (WTN 640H) is seen on 29 September 1986 after being repainted into Confidence livery during the summer holiday.** Trevor Follows

18	VWM 83L	Leyland Atlantean AN68/1R	7204200	H45/29D
		Alexander	AL14/2070/3	
	May 1973	New to Southport Corporation No 83		
	Apr 1974	Merseyside PTE No 83		
	Jan 1984	Renumbered No 0683		
	Aug 1988	**Confidence, Leicester**		
	Sep 2001	P. Weatherby, Southport for preservation		
	May 2019	Unknown owner for continued preservation		

The first two AN68s (Nos 18/19) were part of a batch of ten new to Southport Corporation. The Alexander AL bodies featured newly introduced aluminium alloy construction, front and rear peaked domes, Vee driver's windscreen and a faired-in engine compartment. Following an overhaul and upper deck refurbishment at Merseyside PTE's Edge Lane works in 1979, No 18 was unusual in having scenes of the Merseyside skyline depicted on its upper deck interior cove panels in a bid to reduce graffiti.

The Alexander bodies proved to be extremely well built and robust and No 18 was purchased for preservation by Peter Weatherby; last being used by Confidence on 31 August 2001. It was initially restored into Merseyside PTE Verona Green and cream livery before being returned to its original Southport red and cream colours. A change of ownership occurred in 2019.

19	VWM 89L	Leyland Atlantean AN68/1R	7300046	H45/29D
		Alexander	AL14/2070/9	
	May 1973	New to Southport Corporation No 89		
	Apr 1974	Merseyside PTE No 89		
	Jan 1984	Renumbered No 0689		
	Aug 1988	**Confidence, Leicester**		
	May 2001	J. Robinson, Kimbolton, Cambridgeshire for preservation		
	Jun 2006	Weller, Oxfordshire as a mobile home		
	2009/10	Oldbeth.com mobile home for hire, London		

The background to No 19 is the same as No 18, although it did not feature the Merseyside skyline on the cove panels. No 19 ran its last school service on 4 May 2001 and was collected by John Robinson the next day for preservation. It was quickly repainted into its original red and cream Southport livery and shown in its home town the following August. It was sold in June 2006 for conversion into a mobile home, which took 18 months, before spending two years travelling around Europe. After returning to the UK we believe it was sold around 2009/10 for use as a mobile home for hire in the London area – see 'www.oldbeth.com'.

23	HOR 305N	Leyland Atlantean AN68/1R	7501065	H45/30D
		Alexander	AL40/3773/4	
	May 1975	New to Portsmouth Corporation No 305		
	Oct 1986	Portsmouth City Transport Ltd No 305		
	Jun 1988	Portsmouth Citybus No 305		
	Jan 1990	Southdown Motor Services No 305 but not operated		
	Apr 1991	**Confidence, Leicester**		
	Mar 2002	Littledale, Cosham, Hampshire for preservation		
	Jul 2006	Blair, Upham, Hampshire for continued preservation		
	Sep 2007	Rayner, Portchester, Hampshire for continued preservation		
	Mar 2012	Hampshire Bus & Coach Preservation Group, Winchester for continued preservation		
	Feb 2015	Unknown owner, Brighton		
	Unknown	Exported to Australia – status unknown		

Nos 23 & 24 were both new to City of Portsmouth Passenger Transport Department and had similar Alexander AL type bodies to the former Southport pair but with wrap round windscreens and without the faired in engine panels. The lower deck seating capacity was reduced to 29 in November 1975 when Videmat ticket machines were installed but restored back to 30 when the machines were removed in November/December 1980.

The operation was incorporated on 26 October 1986 in readiness for privatisation by the City Council but the process became protracted. Eventually, on 10 June 1988 PCT Ltd was sold, inter alia, to Portsmouth Citybus Ltd with ultimate ownership split Southampton

With destination blinds set appropriately, No 18 (VWM 83L) is ready for its next journey. It was the first AN68-type Atlantean to join the fleet. Trevor Follows

The next AN68 was No 19 (VWM 89L) which looks different given the front registration number plate is positioned immediately below the windscreen. The two-piece doors are also shown to good effect. Trevor Follows

VWM 89L was initially sold for preservation and was superbly restored back into Southport livery. It was photographed under a threatening sky at Duxford, attending Showbus on 22 September 2002. Adrian Rodgers

City Transport Ltd (75%) and PCT staff (25%). On 24 October 1989 it was sold to Stagecoach Holdings PLC which placed the operation in its Southdown subsidiary from January 1990. However, the Monopolies & Mergers Commission ordered Stagecoach to divest itself of the Portsmouth operations and on 10 January 1991, Transit Holdings took over. Nos 23 & 24 were not part of this deal and were sold soon after to Confidence – both collected from Horsham.

After reliable service with Confidence No 23 was sold for preservation and restored to Portsmouth livery. Sadly it did not survive and we understand it has been exported to Australia although its status and ownership is not yet known.

The background history of No 24 is the same as No 23. After withdrawal No 24 was also sold for preservation and restored to Portsmouth livery. After various owners it did not survive and was last reported as a static bar and restaurant in East Sussex.

24	HOR 306N	Leyland Atlantean AN68/1R	7501198	H45/30D
		Alexander	AL40/3773/5	
Jun 1975	New to Portsmouth Corporation No 306			
Oct 1986	Portsmouth City Transport Ltd No 306			
Jun 1988	Portsmouth Citybus No 306			
Jan 1990	Southdown Motor Services No 306 but not operated			
Apr 1991	Confidence, Leicester			
Oct 2002	Rayner, Portchester, Hampshire for preservation			
Jun 2005	Blair, Bishopstoke, Hampshire for continued preservation			
Apr 2009	Rayner, Portchester, Hampshire for continued preservation			
Oct 2010	Blair, Upham, Hampshire for continued preservation			
Sep 2013	Rayner, Stillwell & Legg, Winchester for continued preservation			
Feb 2015	Mulpeter (Seaford & District), Seaford, East Sussex for continued preservation			
Nov 2015	Broyle Place, Ringmer, East Sussex, Non PSV as static bar			

Right: **HOR 305N was nicely restored as Portsmouth Citybus No 305 and attended an event in its home city on 27 May 2012 to commemorate Portsmouth back in the 1970s. It is appropriately seen about to pass Southdown 547 (PUF 647) which had been Confidence No 1.**
Simon Gill Collection

Below: **The very small fleet numbers will be noted on Confidence 23 (HOR 305N), seen at Aylestone on 4 March 1992.**
Adrian Rodgers

Below right: **Confidence No 24 (HOR 306N) reverted to a larger fleet number on the front. It is seen at Beaumont Leys on 1 November 1994.** Adrian Rodgers

HOR 306N was also preserved but this time in its original Portsmouth City Transport livery. It was seen at Wisley Air Field during a Cobham Bus Museum event on a very wet 2 April 2006. Simon Gill

After withdrawal by Grampian, No 25 passed to East Midland as part of its Frontrunner North West fleet in Manchester which was acquired by Stagecoach Holdings PLC in April 1989. Stagecoach sold the Frontrunner North West business to Drawlane in September 1989 which saw No 25 move south to Portsmouth to join Southdown. When the Monopolies & Mergers Commission ordered Stagecoach to divest itself of the Portsmouth operations,

No 25 passed to Transit Holdings on 10 January 1991 where it ran in the city still in Frontrunner livery. Following withdrawal Confidence collected the bus from Hillsea depot.

It was not purchased for preservation but joined the Midland Routemaster operation at Potterspury, Northamptonshire. After a few months it was parked up on a site at Towcester where it remained until January 2007 when it is thought to have been scrapped.

25	KSA 183P	Leyland Atlantean AN68/1R	7503929	H45/29D
		Alexander	AL44/3473/6	
	Jan 1976	New to Grampian Regional Transport, Aberdeen, No 183		
	Oct 1986	Grampian Regional Transport Ltd, Aberdeen, No 183		
	Aug 1988	Withdrawn by GRT		
	Mar 1989	East Midland Motor Services, Chesterfield No 434		
	Dec 1989	Southdown Motor Services, Portsmouth No 317		
	Jan 1991	Thames Transit Ltd, Oxford No 317		
	May 1991	Withdrawn by Thames Transit		
	Aug 1991	Confidence, Leicester		
	Apr 2003	Taylor T/A Midland Routemaster, Potterspury, Northamptonshire		
	Jul 2003	In store on A5, Towcester as Taylor ceased operations		
	Jan 2007	Gone assumed scrapped		

Photographed outside the Arriva bus garage at Southgate Street, Leicester is Confidence 25 (KSA 183P). It was the newest Alexander-bodied AN68 and originally operated in Aberdeen. Trevor Follows

Nottingham Atlanteans

The Alexander bodies on the first AN68s proved to be extremely well built and robust, so much so that Ken Williams would have dearly loved to get his hands on former Lothian Regional Transport buses but the Local Authority there would only sell their well turned out vehicles for scrap. As a result, Ken was forced to look elsewhere and when another Local Authority owned fleet, Nottingham City Transport, began to withdraw their distinctive 'Nottingham Standard' AN68 models, nine were acquired between March 1989 and September 1994.

The first one, 20 (OTO 540M) was Nottingham's first AN68/1R Atlantean and was bodied by East Lancashire Coachbuilders to a design originally developed for Nottingham by Northern Counties. East Lancs was still building up its order book following a disastrous fire in 1970 that destroyed their factory in Blackburn so their new facilities could easily accommodate Nottingham's order for 46 AN68s.

The 'Nottingham Standard' was a very distinctive design that included an angled destination indicator making it easier to see, high internal ceilings, curved windscreens and upper deck front windows, and a large front bumper to reduce accident damage. These features also improved airflow at the front and reduced reflections on the screens. Despite having two doors, seating capacity was also maximised and parts standardised between different batches and body manufacturers for ease of maintenance.

The OTO-M batch had one less seat downstairs than later deliveries when a 3 bench seat between the doors replaced the original 2 bench type.

They all proved to be very solid, reliable buses and were the mainstay of the Confidence fleet for 10/12 years.

20	OTO 540M	Leyland Atlantean AN68/1R	7302378	H47/30D
		East Lancs	2501	
	Dec 1973	New to Nottingham City Transport No 540		
	Mar 1989	Confidence, Leicester		
	Feb 2001	S. Lowings, Ravenshead for preservation		
	Oct 2001	Notts & Derby Heritage Transport Group, Ravenshead for continued preservation		

Nottingham 540 entered service from Nottingham's Trent Bridge garage on 10 December 1973 where it spent most of its life, mostly on routes to West Bridgford. Initially withdrawn in May 1988 it was stored in Trent Buses' garage on Manvers Street before moving to Bulwell garage. It was relicensed in September 1988 and returned to Trent Bridge garage prior to final withdrawal due to engine failure.

After being purchased for preservation by Simon Lowings of the Notts & Derby Heritage Transport Group it was partly reframed, repanelled and restored to original Nottingham City Transport livery in August 2005.

No 20 has been superbly restored to original condition by Nottingham Heritage Vehicles and was at Wollaton Park, Nottingham on 1 June 2008.
Simon Gill

This page, top: **The first Leyland Atlantean AN68/1R for Nottingham City Transport was No 540 (OTO 540M) and it also became the first Nottingham Atlantean bought by Confidence. No 20 has a full load on this occasion.** Adrian Rodgers

Above: **The Confidence livery suited the body style of the Nottingham Standard as demonstrated by No 21 (GVO 717N).** Adrian Rodgers

Opposite page, top: **After sale for preservation No 22 (OTO 570M) was kept in Confidence livery until it was sadly sold for scrap. Here it was attending an event at Chatsworth House, Derbyshire on 25 June 2006.** Simon Gill

Centre left: **No 22 also attended a bus rally at Sheffield Meadowhall on 20 September 2009. The M1 Tinsley Viaduct is in the background.** Simon Gill

Centre right: **No 26 (OTO 557M) was photographed arriving in Wigston on 22 May 1993. It was sold for preservation but only survived for a year before being exported to Germany.** Adrian Rodgers

Bottom left: **Two Nottingham Standards await the return of their passengers. No 27 (OTO 551M) is the leading bus. It later became a seat store and shield at Wigston depot.** Adrian Rodgers

Bottom right: **The angled, easy to read, front destination blinds stand out well in this view of No 28 (OTO 562M) in Wigston on 2 September 1993.** Adrian Rodgers

21	GVO 717N	Leyland Atlantean AN68/1R	7403611	H47/31D
	East Lancs		4012	
Mar 1975	New to Nottingham City Transport No 597			
Jan 1990	Confidence, Leicester			
Feb 2002	Franks (Fleetline Buses), Thornton, Leicestershire			
Jul 2004	Unknown dealer for scrap			

No 21 was repainted into Confidence livery at Unity Garage, Leicester during the week commencing 9 April 1990.

22	OTO 570M	Leyland Atlantean AN68/1R	7302376	H47/30D
	East Lancs		2531	
Mar 1974	New to Nottingham City Transport No 570			
Jun 1990	Confidence, Leicester			
May 2005	Notts & Derby Heritage Transport Group, Ravenshead for preservation			
Jan 2009	Towle and Campbell, Awsworth, Notts, for continued preservation			
Jun 2011	Nottingham Heritage Vehicles, Mansfield for continued preservation			
Dec 2011	Unknown dealer, Chesterfield for scrap			

When withdrawn in May 2005 No 22 was the last AN68 in service with Confidence after 15 years – only one year less than its original operator. It was sold for preservation and was rallied in Confidence livery before, sadly, going for scrap.

26	OTO 557M	Leyland Atlantean AN68/1R	7304181	H47/30D
	East Lancs		2518	
Feb 1974	New to Nottingham City Transport No 557			
Oct 1992	Confidence, Leicester			
Oct 2002	Heaps, Bradford, West Yorkshire for preservation and kept at the Keighley Bus Museum			
Sep 2003	Carl Ireland (dealer), Hull, East Yorkshire			
Nov 2003	Exported to unknown owner in Germany			

27	OTO 551M	Leyland Atlantean AN68/1R	7302377	H47/30D
	East Lancs		2512	
Jan 1974	New to Nottingham City Transport No 551			
Oct 1992	Confidence, Leicester			
Nov 2000	Withdrawn for use as a shield and seat store at Wigston depot			
Jul 2006	Dismantled and remains sold for scrap.			

No 27 was the first AN68 Atlantean to be taken out of service on 23 November 2000. It replaced No 16 (WTN 640H) as the shield and seat store at Wigston depot until finally being scrapped in July 2006.

28	OTO 562M	Leyland Atlantean AN68/1R	7302758	H47/30D
	East Lancs		2523	
Feb 1974	New to Nottingham City Transport No 562			
Aug 1993	Confidence, Leicester			
Feb 2003	Powell & Watson (Thurmaston Bus), Leicester			
May 2003	Taylor (C&N Travel), Leicester			
Nov 2006	Destroyed by fire during an arson attack at the C&N depot at Barrow upon Soar on Sunday 26 November 2006 and remains sold for scrap			

After use by Confidence No 28 ended up with C&N Travel from May 2003 where it operated in this green and white livery, as seen here on High Street, Barrow upon Soar. It was destroyed by fire in an arson attack at their depot on 26 November 2006. Adrian Rodgers

29	MNU 625P	Leyland Atlantean AN68/1R	7504643		H47/31D
		East Lancs	4714		
	Feb 1976	New to Nottingham City Transport No 625			
	May 1994	**Confidence, Leicester**			
	Oct 2003	Franks (Fleetline Buses), Thornton, Leicestershire			
	Aug 2004	Unknown dealer			
	Nov 2005	Nottingham Heritage Vehicles, Ravenshead, for preservation			
	Jan 2006	Turner, Hucknall, Notts for continued preservation			
	Oct 2009	Nottingham Heritage Vehicles, Ravenshead			
	Oct 2009	Sims Metals, Nottingham, for scrap			

Basking in the sunshine with the centre door open to provide the driver with some ventilation is No 29 (MNU 625P). Adrian Rodgers

30	MNU 631P	Leyland Atlantean AN68/1R	7504651		H47/31D
		East Lancs	4724		
	Mar 1976	New to Nottingham City Transport No 631			
	May 1994	**Confidence, Leicester**			
	May 2002	Renown, Bexhill, East Sussex			
	Apr 2003	Carl Ireland (dealer), Hull, East Yorkshire			
	Jan 2005	Exported to Danny Chabaud, Haute Vienne, France			
	Sep 2005	Unknown Association, North of France			
	Dec 2009	Christophe Mesmacre, Champagne, France			
	Oct 2010	Ponthou Poids Lourd (Scania dealership), Le Mans, France re-registered W-224-AS			

Parked in exactly the same spot but photographed from the other side on another day is No 30 (MNU 631P). Adrian Rodgers

33	MNU 632P	Leyland Atlantean AN68/1R	7504644		H47/31D
		East Lancs	4717		
	Feb 1976	New to Nottingham City Transport No 632			
	Sep 1994	**Confidence, Leicester**			
	Feb 2003	Powell & Watson (Thurmaston Bus), Leicester			
	Apr 2004	Wigley (dealer), Carlton, Barnsley, for scrap			

Looking fresh from repainting in Confidence colours is the last of the Nottingham Atlanteans, No 33 (MNU 632P). Trevor Follows

Leyland Olympian/ East Lancs

The Olympian was launched in 1980 to replace the Leyland Atlantean, Bristol VRT and Daimler Fleetline with the first production examples entering service the following year. Those with chassis numbers below 1000 were built at Bristol with early examples being registered as Bristols. In 1983 production transferred to Workington, Cumbria, and Leyland, Lancashire before moving again to Irvine, Ayrshire from 1992 after the sale of Leyland to Volvo.

Olympians had to appeal to all sectors of the market, especially NBC who, as we shall see later, required ECW low height bodywork. Other manufacturers including Alexander, East Lancs, Leyland, Marshall, Northern Counties, Optare and Roe also built bodies.

Rather than a conventional chassis the Olympian was made up of three modules comprising a front end with front axle, a rear axle and an engine compartment. All were then bolted together utilising a perimeter underframe and 'in-riggers' rather than the usual out-riggers. A choice of engines included the Gardner 6LXB 10.45 litre unit which powered those operated by Confidence. Drive was through an integral fluid-flywheel with five-speed 'Hydracyclic' gearbox incorporating a retarder, with either semi-automatic or fully automatic control. Unlike the Atlantean, air suspension was standard together with dual circuit air brakes.

A total of 5,581 Leyland Olympians were built, of which 1,003 (including prototypes) were made in Bristol and 4,578 at Workington/Leyland. Of these, 1,470 were bodied by ECW, 299 by Roe and only 95 by East Lancs.

38	A511 VKG	Leyland Olympian ONLXB/1R	ON963		H43/31F
		East Lancs	A2915		
	Jan 1984	New to Cardiff City Transport No 511			
	Sep 1998	Munden (dealer), Bristol			
	Sep 1998	**Confidence, Leicester**			
	Jul 2007	Dismantled for spares and remains scrapped			

No 38 was the first of the second batch of Olympians purchased by Cardiff. They were regular performers on service 30 to Newport. In 1997 Cardiff refurbished four Olympians to extend their life in the city but decided it was too costly so disposal was preferred.

No 38 proved very reliable in service and was the first of 22 Leyland Olympians to join the fleet. The East Lancs body was not as robust as the ECW and Roe bodied examples, with rivets becoming loose, which led to it being the first to be withdrawn. It was dismantled for spares before final disposal in July 2007.

39	RBO 510Y	Leyland Olympian ONLXB/1R	ON487		H43/31F
		East Lancs	2904		
	Feb 1983	New to Cardiff City Transport No 510			
	Mar 1999	**Confidence, Leicester**			
	Aug 2008	348 Group, Cardiff for preservation			
	Sep 2010	Cardiff Transport Preservation Group for continued preservation			
	Oct 2010	Jones, Cardiff for continued preservation			
	May 2013	Watts Coaches, Bonvilston, Cardiff			
	Oct 2014	Challenge, London – Non PSV use			

An order for nine Olympians for delivery in August 1982 was put back to early 1983 when No 39 was one of the first to arrive. It, together with Cardiff Nos 502/4/7, was delivered in an experimental livery with black window surrounds on its all over orange livery with a white band between decks. This was not considered a success and standard livery was applied within six months. Lower deck seats were moquette with brown vinyl seats upstairs, those at the rear of the top deck being vandal proof.

In March 1990, it was selected for an upgrade to comply with the Disabled Persons Transport Advisory Committee (DiPTAC) specification, receiving lower entrance steps, non-slip grab rails and a larger luggage pen. This reduced the lower deck seating capacity from 31 to 29. It was used on service 112 from Ely to Trowbridge calling at Heath Hospital. The changes extended its life in the city slightly as it was the last of the batch to be withdrawn.

No 38 was bought direct from Cardiff and the lower deck seating capacity increased back to 31. Enthusiasts in its home city were keen to buy it for preservation but, after several owners, it did not survive and in 2014 was bought by a theatrical group in London.

No 38 (A511 VKG) as seen on 12 October 2001 when it had been in the fleet for three years. When first acquired all Olympians tended to have their front mounted radiator grille painted red, but were later painted black. Adrian Rodgers

No 39 (RBO 510Y) entered service with Confidence still wearing its Cardiff orange and white livery. It is seen here at Wigston depot with AEC Routemaster No 15 (WLT 655). Trevor Follows

Parked at Saffron Lane to allow its passengers to enjoy the Sports Stadium is No 39 on 9 July 2003. Adrian Rodgers

Leyland Olympian/Roe and Optare

We have already looked at the specification of the Leyland Olympian model which was to prove so successful, not only within the wider bus industry but also for Confidence where it became the preferred double deck bus purchase between 1998 and 2012.

Three examples with Roe bodies were acquired, of which one remains in service at the time of writing. Charles H Roe Ltd, to give the firm its full title, was originally established under that name at Cross Gates, Leeds in 1920. After various changes of ownership Roe became part of Leyland in 1965 and was nationalised in 1975. The factory closed in September 1984 but reopened in February 1985 after a new company, Optare, was set up by former employees. Optare went on to body 42 Leyland Olympians to the Roe design.

Unlike the ECW bodies which were usually 13ft 8ins high, these were built to an intermediate height of 14ft 2ins and featured flat instead of wraparound windscreens. The three West Yorkshire PTE buses (UWW 8-10X) were fitted with fare boxes and entered service from Hall Ings garage, Bradford on services 636/637 to Clayton, 640 to Saltaire and 642 to Greengate. They remained in Bradford until just before deregulation as WYPTE decided they had too many buses, so rather than be transferred to Yorkshire Rider they were all withdrawn for disposal on 25 October 1986, having spent their final month in Leeds.

No 46 originally entered service with WYPTE on 12 March 1982. It was repainted in September 1985 and was last used in Bradford on 30 September 1986. It was transferred to Bramley garage in Leeds and entered service there on 2 October 1986; being last used on 25 October 1986 and placed in store at Middleton garage. It had a much longer career with Cambus, operating from their Peterborough and Cambridge garages, before acquisition by Confidence where it remains part of the active fleet.

Opposite page, top left: **When UWW 8X arrived at Cambus it initially operated in West Yorkshire PTE livery with two fleet numbers 505 and 508. No 505 was correct and it is seen outside Deeping St. James garage on 26 April 1987 with No 50 (BNG 886B), a Bristol Lodekka FS5G with ECW H33/27R body, which was used for special duties. It was previously Eastern Counties LFS66.** Peter Cordwell

Top right: **Confidence No 46 (UWW 8X) was the first of three ex-WYPTE Leyland Olympians to arrive. Its various grilles were initially painted red as shown.** Trevor Follows

Centre left: **With all grilles now painted black, No 46 is seen in Whittlesea on 19 May 2019.** Simon Gill

Centre right: **The lower deck with some damaged seat squabs and cushions replaced with a different moquette pattern. Handrails, including those on the top of the seats, have been covered to avoid injury on school work. Interior of the upper deck with matching seats throughout.** Simon Gill

46	UWW 8X	Leyland Olympian ONLXB/1R	ON103		H47/29F
		Roe	G08541		
	Mar 1982	New to West Yorkshire PTE No 5008			
	Oct 1986	Withdrawn by West Yorkshire PTE and placed in store			
	Mar 1987	Cambus, Cambridge No 505			
	Oct 2000	Withdrawn by Cambus, Cambridge			
	Mar 2001	Fleetlink (dealer), Mossley Hill, Liverpool			
	Apr 2001	Confidence, Leicester			

No 505 (UWW 8X) was repainted in the new Cambus livery of dark blue, cream and light blue and is shown departing from Peterborough bus station on 1 October 1988 with the local 'Peterborough & District' name above Cambus. Simon Gill

No 47 originally entered service with WYPTE on 28 March 1982. It was repainted in April 1986 and was last used in Bradford on 3 October 1986. It was transferred to Sovereign Street garage in Leeds and entered service there on 4 October 1986; being last used on 25 October 1986 and placed in store at Middleton garage. Surprisingly, it was reinstated briefly in January 1987 and loaned to Yorkshire Rider from 1 February to 6 February 1987 to cover school services in the Bingley area which were affected by a strike by West Yorkshire Road Car Company drivers.

Since then, it had a varied life beside the seaside in Weymouth with Southern National, followed by the Isle of Man, before acquisition by Confidence. It has now been sold for preservation and was noted still in Confidence livery but carrying Cambus fleet names in May 2019.

Right: **The second operator of UWW 10X was Southern National, albeit the revived fleet that was formed in the run up to the privatisation of Western National, and not the same one that operated No 7 (UOD 500). Allocated No 510 it is seen in Weymouth on 27 June 1989 with the LEYLAND lettering still prominent above the front grille.** Peter Cordwell

47	UWW 10X	Leyland Olympian ONLXB/1R	ON112		H47/29F
		Roe	G08543		
	Mar 1982	New to West Yorkshire PTE No 5010			
	Oct 1986	Withdrawn by West Yorkshire PTE and placed in store			
	Feb 1987	Loaned to Yorkshire Rider (see page 69)			
	Mar 1987	Southern National, Taunton, Somerset No 510			
	Mar 1996	Isle of Man Department of Tourism & Transport No 80 re-registered MAN 80N			
	Dec 1996	Entered service with Isle of Man DofT&T No 80			
	Jul 2001	Ensign (dealer), Purfleet, Essex, re-registered UWW 10X			
	Sep 2001	**Confidence, Leicester**			
	Aug 2018	Thorn, Bromley for preservation			
	Mar 2019	Merryweather & Longmire, Peterborough for continued preservation			

Top: **No 47 (UWW 10X) entered service in Isle of Man Transport livery carrying fleet number 80. Here it leans heavily at Swain Street, Leicester on 29 September 2001.** Adrian Rodgers

Centre left: **No 47 (UWW 10X) looked tidy when attending the rally organised by the Leicester Transport Heritage Trust and Great Central Railway at Quorn & Woodhouse station on 21 April 2018.** Simon Gill

Centre right: **The nearside rear of the Roe body is very similar to the ECW body, although it is slightly taller.** Simon Gill

Bottom: **No 47 was sold for preservation in August 2018 and following a change of owner it was running at Whittlesea on 19 May 2019 displaying 'Cambus' fleet names on the sides.** Simon Gill

Opposite page: **A posed photo during an enthusiasts' tour sees No 53 near Wigston Harcourt on 16 May 2009. The slight damage to the roof panels proves these buses are slightly taller than the ECW-bodied examples.** Simon Gill

53	UWW 9X	Leyland Olympian ONLXB/1R	ON111		H47/29F
		Roe	G08542		
	Mar 1982	New to West Yorkshire PTE No 5009			
	Oct 1986	Withdrawn by West Yorkshire PTE and placed in store			
	Apr 1987	Southern National, Taunton, Somerset No 509			
	Mar 1996	Isle of Man Department of Tourism & Transport No 45 re-registered CMN 45C			
	Jul 1996	Entered service with Isle of Man DofT&T No 45			
	Jul 2001	Ensign (dealer), Purfleet, Essex, re-registered UWW 9X			
	Nov 2001	Forestdale Coaches, Addington, Buckinghamshire			
	Apr 2002	**Confidence, Leicester**			
	Nov 2017	Stazicker (dealer), Rawdon, Leeds – registration UWW 9X kept			
	Jan 2018	Mobile caravan / Fishermans hut, Wales			

54	E157 OMD	Leyland Olympian ONLXB/1RH	ON10644		H47/29F
		Optare	309		
	Apr 1988	New to Boro'line, Maidstone, Kent No 757			
	Feb 1992	Kentish Bus, Crayford, Bexley, Kent No 757			
	Nov 1997	Arriva Kent Thameside, Dartford, Kent No 5757			
	Jan 1999	Arriva Kent & Sussex, Sheerness, Kent No 5757			
	May 2002	**Confidence, Leicester**			
	Aug 2018	Boxall, Bromley for preservation			

No 53 originally entered service with WYPTE on 12 March 1982. It was repainted in September 1985 and was last used in Bradford on 2 October 1986. It was transferred to Bramley garage in Leeds and entered service there on 3 October 1986; being last used on 24 October 1986 and placed in store at Middleton garage.

Since then, it had a varied life beside the seaside in Weymouth with Southern National, followed by the Isle of Man, before being operated briefly by Forestdale Coaches of Addington, moving to Confidence five months later. Initial reports suggesting it had been acquired for preservation proved wrong and it was last reported as a Fishermans hut in Wales.

In January 1988 Boro'line Maidstone entered the London Regional Transport tendering scene having won three routes in the Chislehurst and Sidcup area. It operated from the Bexley Council depot at Crayford and ordered 14 ECW-bodied Leyland Olympians but these were not delivered in time. Instead, eleven Optare-bodied Olympians, which were originally built as stock vehicles for Optare, including No 54, were purchased by Maidstone. It received a striking livery of blue and yellow with silver-grey skirt and red flash-line.

By 1991, Boro'line's finances were in a difficult position so Kentish Bus bought the London operations in February 1992, including these Olympians; the remainder falling into Receivership. The livery changed to primrose and maroon and the operation moved to Dartford. The operation was taken over by Arriva Kent & Sussex at Sheerness which then became Arriva Medway Towns in January 2001. No 54 remained unique in the Confidence fleet and was sold for preservation after 16 years' reliable service.

Above: **Looking particularly smart whilst parked in the middle of Humberstone Gate, before the area was remodelled, is No 54 (E157 OMD). It was the newest Leyland Olympian to be operated and the only one with an Optare body – the successor to Roe.** Simon Gill

Left: **Jockeying for road position in Humberstone Gate with two First Leicester buses is No 54 (E157 OMD).** Simon Gill

Opposite page, top: **Confidence No 42 entered service carrying the Oxford Travelwise advertisement with the front in Worths of Enstone Livery. It was photographed near Wigston depot on 17 April 2000.**

Bottom left: **Keeping with the dual door tradition of the Leyland Atlanteans, No 42 was used for over four years with the centre door sealed, as seen in Evington on 13 September 2002.**

Bottom right: **You can't see the join! The centre doors were removed and the gap rebuilt in the summer of 2004. You would never know as No 42 demonstrates at Abbey Meadows on 5 May 2005.**
All three: Adrian Rodgers

Leyland Olympian/ECW

With 16 examples joining the fleet, this is the most common sort of bus operated by Confidence over the past fifty years which has not gone unnoticed by those interested in the type. We have already looked at the essential details of the Leyland Olympian underframe, so here we appreciate the importance of Eastern Coach Works (ECW) bodies built in Lowestoft until the factory was closed by Leyland at the end of January 1987.

Construction of coach bodies began in 1919 when a garage and workshop opened on the site in Lowestoft. Eastern Coach Works Ltd came into being on 1 July 1936 as a Tilling & British Automobile Traction Group subsidiary. After the Second World War intervened, production resumed in February 1946 and grew rapidly as the need for new buses escalated. Following the then Labour Government's nationalisation of much of the transport industry the Tilling Group, including ECW, came under state control via the British Transport Commission (BTC) on 1 January 1948. This resulted in its products, and those of chassis manufacturer Bristol, no longer being available to non-nationalised operators. This was reversed from 1967 following an exchange of shares between the Transport Holding Company (THC as successor to BTC) and the Leyland Group.

With ECW being renowned for quality, it did not take long to gain new customers, in addition to supplying the nationalised operators which increased when the National Bus Company (NBC) was formed on 1 January 1969 to take over the THC and the private British Electric Traction Group. Production boomed in the 1970s and early 1980s with operators keen to take advantage of a New Bus Grant which subsidised the cost of new buses by as much as 50%.

The Olympian replaced the ECW-bodied Bristol VRT as the NBC's main double deck bus. Most were 31ft 5ins (9.57m) long 77-seaters with a standard height of 13ft 8ins (4.16m), although City of Oxford was unusual in specifying a dual door layout with

centrally positioned staircase. London Transport's were also dual door and featured split level front entrance steps and low profile tyres requiring smaller wheel arches.

Confidence has operated some particularly noteworthy examples including No 52 (EEH 904Y) with a unique top deck, No 58 (JFR 5W) the 20th one built and No 65 (A132 SMA) the second chassis built at Workington.

No 42 operated in Oxford and carried two overall advertisements, one was blue based for Cumnor Hill Garage (MotorLux Volvo) with a later for one for Travelwise. Confidence initially sealed the centre door before rebuilding it in their workshops. It was dismantled on site and remains sold for scrap.

42	VJO 205X	Leyland Olympian ONLXB/1R	ON257	H47/31F
		ECW	25142	
	Jun 1982	New to City of Oxford Motor Services No 205 as H47/28D		
	Sep 1999	Worth, Enstone, Oxfordshire		
	Mar 2000	**Confidence, Leicester**		
	Sep 2004	Converted to H47/31F by Confidence		
	Feb 2013	Scrapped		

Initially allocated to Gallowgate, Newcastle garage, United's No 224 was transferred to Scarborough in July 1986 before moving to a new company, Northumbria Motor Services, on 7 September when United was split in two in readiness for privatisation. It was renumbered 414 on 30 November 1986 and allocated to Hexham.

In November 1990 it was involved in a vehicle exchange with Kentish Bus and was allocated to Northfleet. A further move in December 1995 saw No 48 in North Wales with Arriva Cymru, initially at Wrexham before transferring to Bangor in April 1998, followed by Corwen in March 1999. It was withdrawn in June 2001, passing to Confidence via Fleetlink (dealer).

No 48 gave good service and was withdrawn in October 2014 passing to a dealer for scrap.

44	FUM 490Y	Leyland Olympian ONLXB/1R		ON653		H45/29F
		ECW		25551		
	Apr 1983	New to West Yorkshire Road Car Company, Harrogate, No 1815 seating H45/32F				
	Jan 1988	Re-seated to CH41/29F by Optare				
	Aug 1989	Keighley & District, Keighley, No 1815				
	Jan 1990	Renumbered 361 by Keighley & District				
	Dec 1993	Re-seated to H41/29F				
	Jan 1996	Re-seated to H45/29F				
	Dec 2000	Fleetmaster (dealer), Horsham, West Sussex on paper only				
	Dec 2000	**Confidence, Leicester**				
	Mar 2008	Dismantled for spares and remains scrapped at Wigston depot				

No 44 was new to West Yorkshire's Leeds garage for bus services. It was despatched to local coachbuilder Optare on 15 December 1987 to have coach seats fitted on both decks, being the second of twelve Olympians chosen to upgrade the long, prestigious 36 route from Leeds to Ripon via Harrogate. It returned to service the following month. With the demise of West Yorkshire Road Car Company after 12 August 1989 an exchange of vehicles took place and No 1815 was transferred to Keighley.

In January 1990 it was renumbered 361 and was the first dual purpose Olympian to receive Keighley & District's new chinchilla and red livery. Various seating changes took place before sale to Confidence where it retained coach seats on the lower deck. Its early demise was due to chassis corrosion.

48	AEF 224Y	Leyland Olympian ONLXB/1R		ON736		H45/32F
		ECW		25533		
	May 1983	New to United Automobile Company, Darlington No 224				
	Sep 1986	Northumbria Motor Services, Newcastle No 224				
	Nov 1986	Renumbered 414 by Northumbria				
	Nov 1990	Kentish Bus, Northfleet No 305				
	Feb 1995	Renumbered 605 by Kentish Bus				
	Dec 1995	Arriva Cymru, Bangor No DOG224				
	Jul 2001	Fleetmaster (dealer), Horsham, West Sussex on paper only				
	Sep 2001	**Confidence, Leicester**				
	Oct 2014	Withdrawn by Confidence				
	Apr 2015	Wigley (dealer), Carlton, Barnsley for scrap				

49	XWY 476X	Leyland Olympian ONLXB/1R		ON300		H45/32F
		ECW		25222		
	May 1982	New to West Riding Automobile Company, Wakefield No 476				
	Nov 1982	Renumbered 501 by West Riding				
	Jul 1987	Metrobus, Orpington				
	Dec 1995	Isle of Man Department of Tourism & Transport No 82 re-registered DMH 82H				
	Mar 1996	Entered service with Isle of Man DofT&T No 82				
	Jul 2001	Ensign (dealer), Purfleet, Essex and re-registered XWY 476X				
	Sep 2001	**Confidence, Leicester**				
	Sep 2018	Corcoran, Streatham for preservation				

The bus of many colours! As West Riding No 476 in NBC poppy red livery with a white band and MetroBus logos, it entered service on 12 May 1982 at Castleford garage. When West Riding decided to number the Olympians in a new series it was renumbered 501 on 7 November 1982. A loan to Selby garage on 30 March 1985 resulted in a permanent transfer by May although it returned to Castleford in September 1985.

At that time West Yorkshire PTE required all buses operating in the area to be in their livery so it was repainted Verona green and cream in May 1986. As WYPTE ceased to be an operator this did not last long as in February 1987 it was repainted into the newly privatised West Riding red and cream livery with Castleford fleet names.

Surprisingly, it was withdrawn the following June and sold to the relatively new operator, Metrobus of Orpington for use on London outer zone routes, receiving their blue and yellow livery. Another sale in December 1995 saw it move to the Isle of Man, entering service in March 1996. After service on the island No 49 was acquired by Confidence in September 2001 where it was used in IoM livery until it could be repainted.

A new lower deck floor was fitted and it gave Confidence great service before being bought by a member of the Bromley Bus Preservation Group for preservation.

Top: No 48 (AEF 224Y) took part in an enthusiasts' tour on 16 May 2009 and is seen near Wigston depot. It is a typical ECW-bodied Leyland Olympian of the 1980s. Simon Gill

Centre left: Seen at Leeds, City Square on 24 July 1982 in original condition, with MetroBus West Riding fleet name, is No 476 (XWY 476X). It was renumbered 501 three months later. Peter Cordwell

Centre right: After its various liveries with West Riding, XWY 476X moved to Metrobus, Orpington and was repainted blue and yellow. It was on service 356 to Biggin Hill on 24 January 1991. Simon Gill Collection

Bottom left: No 49 (XWY 476X) entered service in full Isle of Man Transport livery with fleet number 82. It was photographed on 15 September 2001 when newly acquired. Adrian Rodgers

Bottom right: Almost in the same spot we see No 49 after being fully repainted in Confidence livery with red grilles. Trevor Follows

51	EEH 903Y	Leyland Olympian ONLXB/1R	ON713		H45/32F
	ECW		25627		
Jul 1983	New to Midland Red (North), Cannock No 1903				
Apr 1998	Arriva Midlands North, Cannock No 1903				
Mar 2000	Stevensons, Uttoxeter No 1903				
Nov 2001	Withdrawn by Stevensons, Uttoxeter				
Jan 2002	**Confidence, Leicester**				
Mar 2011	Dismantled for spares and remains scrapped at Wigston depot				

52	EEH 904Y	Leyland Olympian ONLXB/1R	ON749		H45/32F
	ECW		25628		
Jun 1983	New to Midland Red (North), Cannock No 1904				
Jul 1993	C-Line, Manchester No 1904				
Jan 1994	Midland Red (North), Cannock No 1904				
Jan 1995	Stevensons, Uttoxeter No 86				
Jun 1996	Renumbered 1904 by Stevensons				
Apr 1997	Withdrawn following accident damage				
Oct 1997	Reinstated after repairs by Stevensons No 1904				
Jan 2001	Arriva Midlands North, Cannock No 1904				
Dec 2001	Withdrawn by Arriva Midlands North				
Feb 2002	**Confidence, Leicester**				
Aug 2014	Withdrawn and being dismantled for spares				
Feb 2020	Being used for spares				

When Midland Red was split up in September 1981 Midland Red (North) abandoned the old name in favour of local identity names on a colour unique to each area. Its first new buses were ten Olympians, including No 1903 which carried a red livery with green band below the lower deck windows and 'Mercian' fleet name denoting it was allocated to Tamworth garage.

A red and white livery was introduced in 1992 and, in April that year, No 1903 was transferred to Cannock garage. Once Arriva assumed control, it was transferred to the associated Stevensons fleet at Swadlincote in March 2000, moving to Burton-upon-Trent the following September before being withdrawn in November 2001.

Acquired by Confidence in January 2002, it was a trusty member of the fleet before being withdrawn and scrapped in March 2011.

Above: **No 51 (EEH 903Y) was another of the Leyland Olympians used on the enthusiasts' tour on 16 May 2009. It is shown having returned to Wigston depot on that occasion.** Simon Gill

Right: **Stevensons 1904 (EEH 904Y) has just received the roof from prototype Leyland Olympian No 99 (Q246 FVT) parked alongside it at Uttoxeter garage in 1997. Ray Buckley is on the top of No 99.** Eric Wain

No 55 was new to London Transport (LT) as L71 in May 1986. It was initially stored at Plumstead garage, entering service the following month at Bexleyheath garage. In August 1986 it moved to Plumstead and remained in service there through two changes of ownership via Selkent (when LT was split up for privatisation) and Stagecoach, when the transport group acquired some London operators. With the introduction of low floor buses, like Confidence No 72, it was withdrawn in June 1999 and passed to Ensign who converted it to single door for onward sale to the Isle of Man.

After use in the IoM it was acquired by Confidence and has been a reliable member of the fleet. The small wheel arches and low profile tyres caused a problem with grounding so these have been rebuilt to the more conventional layout. No 55 was delicensed towards the end of 2018 but was reinstated to the operational fleet in September 2019.

No 52 is not all it seems! Like No 51 it was new to Midland Red (North)'s (MRN) Tamworth garage where it remained for ten years. In July 1993 it was transferred to the associated C-Line operation in Macclesfield which MRN had inherited from Crosville. It remained at Macclesfield in January 1994 when the C-Line licences were transferred to MRN and, again, in January 1995 when the associated Stevensons took over operations in the town.

Disaster struck in April 1997 when it was involved in a collision with a low bridge which decapitated the top deck. It was rebuilt by Ray Buckley by transferring the top deck from the first prototype Olympian with a Bristol VRT front, chassis no B45-01 registered Q246 FVT, which Stevensons had acquired as an unfinished shell in June 1983. After extensive rebuilding the prototype entered service in January 1985 as No 99. With a new roof fitted, No 1904 returned to service at Macclesfield in October 1997 before moving to Arriva Midlands North at Winsford in January 2001.

After final withdrawal it was bought by Confidence in February 2002. Little was known about its history until it was time to repair a smashed upper deck window – a standard window wouldn't fit as the prototype had a different size to the production models! At the time of writing No 52 remains in stock and is being used for spares.

55	C71 CHM	Leyland Olympian ONLXB/1RH	ON2353		H42/30F
	ECW		26353		
May 1986	New to London Transport No L71 as H42/26D				
Apr 1989	South East London & Kent Bus Company (Selkent) No L71				
Sep 1994	Stagecoach Selkent No L71				
Jun 1999	Ensign (dealer), Purfleet, Essex				
Dec 1999	Isle of Man Department of Tourism & Transport No 11 re-registered EMN 211U, converted to H42/30F by Ensign				
Jan 2000	Entered service with Isle of Man DofT&T No 11				
Jun 2002	Ensign (dealer), Purfleet, Essex and re-registered C71 CHM				
Jul 2002	Confidence, Leicester				
	Still in use				

Enthusiasts wait to depart in No 55 on the latest stage of their 'Olympian' tour on 16 May 2009. Simon Gill

Above: **Despite some dirt on the lower panels caused by earlier rain, No 57 (A139 SMA) still looks smart during the same tour on 16 May 2009.** Simon Gill

Left: **By August 2019, No 57 was being stripped for spares at Wigston depot. 'VOR' written in the rear window means 'Vehicle off Road' – it definitely is before its final journey to the scrap yard – under tow.** Simon Gill

Opposite page: **The grade 2 listed Preston bus station is the location of Stagecoach Ribble No 2105 (JFR 5W) on 9 May 1990.** Joe Gornall

No 58 (JFR 5W) was initially used by Confidence in Burnley & Pendle school bus yellow before being repainted. Adrian Rodgers

Repainting complete and No 58 is seen in Wigston once again. Trevor Follows

57	A139 SMA	Leyland Olympian ONLXB/1R	ON1009	H45/32F
	ECW		25380	
	Nov 1983	New to Crosville Motor Services, Chester No DOG139		
	Nov 1989	North Western Road Car, Liverpool No 657		
	Mar 1995	Liverline, Liverpool No 657		
	Oct 1997	North Western Road Car, Liverpool No 657		
	Apr 1998	Arriva North West, Liverpool No 657		
	Apr 2000	Arriva Midlands North, Cannock No 1957		
	Mar 2002	Withdrawn by Arriva Midlands North		
	Sep 2002	Reinstated by Arriva Midlands North, Cannock No 1957		
	Nov 2002	**Confidence, Leicester**		
	Feb 2020	Still owned and being dismantled for spares		

This bus was new to the original Crosville Motor Services Company and operated from Rock Ferry depot before moving to Runcorn in October 1987. Following privatisation of the NBC and sale to Drawlane Group, Crosville was split up and the operations in Runcorn were absorbed into the relatively new North Western Road Car (NWRC) company in November 1989. After the acquisition of Liverline, which became a brand of NWRC, No 57 moved there before returning to NWRC. The operation was re-branded Arriva North West in 1998 and it moved to Winsford, staying there under Arriva Midlands North before moving to Cannock in April 2002.

The bus has given good service to Confidence and is currently in the final stages of being dismantled to provide spares for the remaining Leyland Olympians in the fleet and to help preservation groups with similar buses.

58	JFR 5W	Leyland Olympian ONLXB/1R	ON20	H45/32F
	ECW		24952	
	Jul 1981	New to Ribble Motor Services, Preston No 2105		
	Apr 1989	Stagecoach Ribble, Preston No 2105		
	Apr 2001	Burnley & Pendle, Burnley No 2105		
	Feb 2003	**Confidence, Leicester**		
	Aug 2008	Withdrawn and dismantled for spares		
	Mar 2009	Remains scrapped at Wigston depot		

No 58 was only the 20th Olympian to roll off the production line, entering Ribble service in NBC poppy red livery with a white band at Morecambe garage. On 21 April 1989 Ribble was acquired by Stagecoach Holdings and their striped livery on a white background was eventually applied to No 2105. Garage moves saw it at Clitheroe in January 1990, Preston in July 1992 and Chorley in November 1993. Stagecoach had acquired the Burnley & Pendle municipal operation in 1997 and in May 2000 incorporated it within Stagecoach Ribble. In April 2001 it sold the Burnley operation to Blazefield Holdings and transferred older buses into the town, including No 2105 which retained the same fleet number.

In September 2002, No 2105 was repainted all over yellow as part of the school bus fleet and it remained in this livery for a while after sale to Confidence, until a repaint in black and grey was possible.

No 61 was the second former City of Oxford (COMS) Olympian to be acquired; this time direct from COMS. Apart from a short period at High Wycombe garage in September 1999, we believe it spent most of its life running around the streets of Oxford until acquired by Confidence. In 1997 it carried an all over advert for ComTel. It was loaned to Metrobus during their takeover of operations at Crawley and operated from Godstone garage.

After being bought by Confidence its centre door was sealed until it was converted to single door in the company's own workshop. It remains in service at the time of writing.

61	CUD 221Y	Leyland Olympian ONLXB/1R	ON448		H47/31F
	ECW		25158		
Jan 1983	New to City of Oxford Motor Services No 221 as H47/28D				
Apr 2001	On loan to Metrobus, Orpington				
May 2001	Returned to City of Oxford Motor Services No 221				
Oct 2003	Confidence, Leicester				
Apr 2005	Converted to H47/31F by Confidence				
	Still in use				

63	A502 EJF	Leyland Olympian ONLXB/1R	ON888		H45/32F
	ECW		25519		
Oct 1983	New to Midland Red (East), Leicester No 4502				
Jan 1984	Midland Fox, Leicester No 4502				
Apr 1998	Arriva Fox County, Leicester No 4501				
Sep 2004	Ensign (dealer), Purfleet, Essex on paper only				
Sep 2004	Confidence, Leicester				
Dec 2014	Leicester Transport Heritage Trust for preservation				

Olympian No 63 has spent its whole life in Leicester. A Certificate of Initial Fitness was issued on 18 August 1983 confirming a passenger capacity of 91 in H45/32F configuration with 14 standing. It was delivered in all over light brown undercoat and was probably one of three Olympians noted in Southgate Street depot on Wednesday 24 August 1983. It was then despatched to the former Midland Red Carlyle Road works in Birmingham for painting

into a new livery of yellow front sloping after the first third of the bus, to red on the remaining two thirds. It was delivered at the end of September and, in common with many Olympians built in Bristol, it was registered as a Bristol on 1 October 1983; being one of five of the batch of ten licensed that day, the others being 4501, 4503, 4505 and 4506. These Olympians were the first new buses to be delivered to Midland Red (East) Ltd since the split from Midland Red on 6 September 1981. Luminator electronic destination displays were fitted.

No 4502 was the second of the batch to be put on the road in early October 1983, which was three months prior to the launch of Midland Fox which had been deferred by three months. It therefore took to the road with small Midland Red fleet names which were replaced by large Midland Fox logos when the new

name was launched on 15 January 1984. It was initially allocated to Leicester Southgates Garage before being transferred to Coalville in October 1984, where it was destined to spend the next 20 years. After 9 years in standard fleet livery, the rest of its life was spent in various Leicestershire County Council Safety message overall advertisements, so it never carried Arriva livery.

It was withdrawn in July 2004 and sold to Ensign but was immediately purchased by Confidence and entered service in September 2004 still in LCC livery. The black and grey livery was applied by early 2005. Upon withdrawal Ken Williams kindly donated it to the Leicester Transport Heritage Trust, where he is a member. It was collected by LTHT on Saturday 29 November 2014 having been in service until the day before. A full restoration and eventual return into Midland Fox livery began in 2019.

Opposite page, top: **Another bus to enter service in its former operator's livery was No 61 (CUD 221Y). It is seen at the Meridian complex on 19 December 2003 in COMS livery. Note the rectangular headlamps which make it stand out from the others.** Adrian Rodgers

Bottom: **The neat conversion to single door can be seen on No 61, parked at Quorn & Woodhouse station of the Great Central Railway on 23 April 2016. Inset: Lower deck interior of No 61 shows where the centre door has been rebuilt and the gap fitted with an inwards facing bench seat opposite the stairs.** Simon Gill

This page, top: **Nearly new Midland Red East No 4502 (A502 EJF) is loading at the bottom of Charles Street, Leicester on 22 October 1983 before heading for Thurnby Lodge. The route had been operated by BMMO D9s only four years earlier.** Simon Gill

Right: **Gleaming in its new Confidence livery, No 63 is seen at the familiar spot in Wigston.** Trevor Follows

Above left: When A132 SMA was acquired by Midland Fox it was initially used in Crosville Wales livery, allocated to the Loughborough Coach & Bus operation which had been acquired from Leicester CityBus. It is seen departing from St. Margaret's bus station for Loughborough on 1 April 1989. Simon Gill

Above right: After repainting in Midland Fox livery, No 4516 is seen in Charles Street, Leicester loading for Wigston Harcourt on 22 October 1991. Simon Gill

Right: Parked at Walkers Stadium on 27 July 2009, awaiting the return of its passengers from an Athletics event, is No 65 (A132 SMA). Adrian Rodgers

Below: The classic rear of an ECW-bodied Leyland Olympian shown on No 65. Simon Gill

65	A132 SMA	Leyland Olympian ONLXB/1R	ON1002	H45/32F
		ECW	25733	
	Sep 1983	New to Crosville Motor Services, Chester No DOG132		
	May 1989	Midland Fox, Leicester No 4516		
	Apr 1998	Arriva Fox County, Leicester No 4516		
	Sep 2004	Withdrawn by Arriva Fox County		
	Aug 2005	**Confidence, Leicester**		
	Aug 2010	Withdrawn and dismantled for spares		
	Oct 2010	Remains to Wigston Car Breakers, Wigston for scrap		

This was the second Olympian to come off the Leyland production line at Workington following the decision to close the Bristol factory. It entered service with Crosville at their Caernarfon depot following a decision to demonstrate some investment in new buses in North Wales as most tended to be allocated to garages in the Wirral area.

Unfortunately, this was short lived and, in May 1989, it was transferred to Midland Fox where it was allocated to Loughborough, as part of the Loughborough Coach & Bus Company fleet, before transfer to Wigston by March 1990. Between July 1992 and April 2000 it carried a rear end advertisement for Regency Pine Studios. A final transfer to Leicester, Southgate Street in April 2004 preceded its withdrawal the following September.

Acquired by Confidence in August 2005 it only lasted five years before being dismantled for spares and its remains sold for scrap.

67	BBW 216Y	Leyland Olympian ONLXB/1R	ON354	H47/31F
		ECW	25153	
	Oct 1982	New to City of Oxford Motor Services No 216 as H47/28D		
	Sep 1999	Worth, Enstone, Oxfordshire		
	Jul 2006	**Confidence, Leicester**		
	Feb 2007	Entered service with Confidence converted to H47/31F		
	Oct 2014	Withdrawn and dismantled for spares		
	Dec 2016	Remains sold for scrap		

The third City of Oxford Olympian to join the fleet was another one from Worths of Enstone who have supplied a number of vehicles to Confidence. Once again, we believe it spent its entire life in Oxford before disposal to Worths.

Confidence initially bought No 67 for spares only but it was prepared for service from December 2006, converted from H47/28D to H47/31F and entered service in February 2007. Upon withdrawal it was dismantled for spares and its remains sold for scrap.

69	B187 BLG	Leyland Olympian ONLXB/1R	ON1637	H45/32F
		ECW	26053	
	Dec 1984	New to Crosville Motor Services, Chester No DOG187		
	Aug 1986	Crosville Wales, Bangor No DOG187		
	May 1990	Midland Fox, Leicester No 4527		
	Apr 1998	Arriva Fox County, Leicester No 4527		
	Oct 2006	Ensign (dealer), Purfleet, Essex		
	Dec 2006	Taylor (T/A C&N Travel), Barrow upon Soar, Leicestershire		
	Mar 2008	**Confidence, Leicester**		
		Still in use		

Confidence No 67 (BBW 216Y) was initially purchased for spares but the centre door was removed and it was put into service in February 2007. On 4 May 2010 it was on a private hire to Beaumanor Hall. Adrian Rodgers

After service with Midland Fox/Arriva B187 BLG was acquired by C&N Travel of Barrow upon Soar. It is seen in their green and white livery. Adrian Rodgers

No 69 (B187 BLG) remains a member of the fleet and was photographed at St. Margaret's bus station on a hot 27 July 2016. Adrian Rodgers

After being new to the original Crosville Company and allocated to Pwllheli garage, it remained there when the company was split up on 10 August 1986 and became part of Crosville Wales which started operations that day. By January 1990 it was working from Mold garage before being withdrawn and sold to Midland Fox in May 1990. It was allocated to Coalville garage and remained there until sale to Ensign (dealer).

It was purchased by C&N Travel of Barrow upon Soar to operate schools services. Unfortunately, C&N ceased operations on 29 February 2008 following the death of the founder in December 2007. It remains in use today.

70	B190 BLG	Leyland Olympian ONLXB/1R	ON1687		H45/32F
		ECW	26056		
Jan 1985	New to Crosville Motor Services, Chester No DOG190				
Aug 1986	Crosville Wales, Bangor No DOG190				
May 1990	Midland Fox, Leicester No 4528				
Apr 1998	Arriva Fox County, Leicester No 4528				
Oct 2006	Ensign (dealer), Purfleet, Essex				
Dec 2006	Taylor (T/A C&N Travel), Barrow upon Soar, Leicestershire				
Mar 2008	**Confidence, Leicester**				
	Still in use				

No 70's background is similar to No 69. New to the original Crosville Company, it was allocated to Wrexham garage and remained there when the company was split up on 10 August 1986 and became part of Crosville Wales which started operations that day. By January 1990 it was working from Llandudno Junction garage before being withdrawn and sold to Midland Fox in May 1990. It was allocated to Leicester, Southgate Street garage, moving to Thurmaston in May 1996, then Wigston in April 1998. After the formation of Arriva Fox County it moved to Stamford in October 2000 before returning to Thurmaston by April 2004, followed by Coalville, joining No 69, in April 2006.

After sale to Ensign (dealer) it was purchased by C&N Travel of Barrow upon Soar to operate schools services. Unfortunately, C&N ceased operations on 29 February 2008 following the death of the founder in December 2007. It remains in use today.

76	D137 FYM	Leyland Olympian ONLXB/1RH	ON2420		H42/29F
		ECW	26462		
Sep 1986	New to London Transport No L137 as H42/26D				
Mar 1987	Placed in store at Plumstead garage and later Chiswick Works				
May 1987	Reinstated at Plumstead garage				
Apr 1989	South East London & Kent Bus Company (Selkent) No L137				
Jul 1992	Placed in store after a collision				
Nov 1992	Returned to service at Plumstead garage after repair				
Sep 1994	Stagecoach Selkent No L137				
Jun 1999	Stagecoach Midland Red – Midland Red (South) – No 837 as H42/29F				
Jan 2003	Renumbered 14387 by Stagecoach Midland Red				
Oct 2008	Ellie Rose Travel, Hull, East Yorkshire				
Nov 2012	**Confidence, Leicester**				
	Still in use				

New to London Transport (LT) as L137 in September 1986 it was stored at Plumstead garage before entering service there the following month. It was out of service for an unknown reason between March and May 1987 which entailed a visit to Chiswick Works, possibly for repair. In July 1992 it was involved in a head-on collision with a car whilst working on route 180 so was again delicensed, returning to traffic in November 1992.

With low floor buses replacing Olympians at Plumstead it was transferred, within the Stagecoach Group, to Midland Red (South) in June 1999 and converted to front entrance. It entered service at Nuneaton garage before transferring to Rugby in February 2001. Withdrawn in October 2008 it was sold to Ellie Rose Travel, Hull who ran it until sale to Confidence in November 2012 where it remains in use.

Below left: **Another bus at an Athletics event at Walkers Stadium on 30 July 2009 was No 70 (B190 BLG). It remains part of the current fleet.** Adrian Rodgers

Below: **The final Leyland Olympian to join the fleet was No 76 (D137 FYM). It was new to London Transport but also operated in the Midlands when it was transferred, by Stagecoach, to their Midland Red (South) subsidiary. It looked particularly smart when seen travelling along Saffron Lane on 16 June 2015.** Adrian Rodgers

Leyland Tigers

The Leyland Tiger was introduced in 1982 to replace the successful Leyland Leopard which had been in production for over 20 years with upgrades along the way. Fitted with the more powerful Leyland TL11 engine (most built after 1983 were 245 bhp), air suspension, air brakes and a front mounted radiator, it was designed to counter competition from Volvo and others trying to gain a foothold in the market. As the first new model aimed specifically at high speed motorway running, it was an immediate success and sold well until dropped by Volvo in 1991, after the acquisition of Leyland, as it was unnecessary competition for the B10M. Most chassis received coach bodies with only some bodied as buses.

Of the eight Tigers acquired by Confidence all had Hydracyclic gearboxes except No 43 which had a ZF synchromesh unit. The four Tigers from City of Oxford were operated by that company on the busy X90 'City Link' motorway express from Oxford to London that, in various guises, ran for 92 years until closure on 4 January 2020.

The Ogle-designed Plaxton Paramount was introduced in 1982 to succeed the Supreme. The 3200 was 3.2m high and the 3500 was 3.5m high; both having a waistline sloped forward at the front with a short window, known as a 'feature window', behind the front wheel. A Mk II version followed in 1985. Production ended in 1991 when the Premier and Excalibur were introduced. The Duple Laser replaced the Dominant and was only built between 1982 and 1985.

The first Leyland Tiger, No 41 (A118 PBW), with a high floor Plaxton Paramount 3500 Express body, entered service in the livery of Worth's of Enstone. It is seen near Wigston depot on a misty winter's day in early 2000. Adrian Rodgers

No 43 (C248 CKH) is seen leading a fine line up of three Confidence coaches at Beaumanor Hall, Leicestershire on 19 June 2001 – all in different liveries. It initially retained Hornsby livery which was not too dissimilar to the grey Confidence colours. Adrian Rodgers

After repainting in red and black No 43 still looked very smart. Note the coach style door differs from the two-piece 'express' doors fitted to No 41. Adrian Rodgers

41	A118 PBW	Leyland Tiger TRCTL11/3RH	8400242		C51F
		Plaxton Paramount 3500 Express	8412LTH1X504		
	Jun 1984	New to City of Oxford Motor Services No 118 as C50F			
	Jul 1996	Worth, Enstone, Oxfordshire			
	Aug 1996	Re-seated to C51F			
	Jan 2000	**Confidence, Leicester**			
	Oct 2013	Scrapped			

As with all the City of Oxford coaches this would have had a hard life on express services into London for 12 years. The high floor Plaxton Paramount 3500 body was unusual in having folding express doors, as most high floor coaches tended to be built for touring work.

43	C248 CKH	Leyland Tiger TRCTL11/3RZ	8401085		C49FT
		Plaxton Paramount II 3500	8512LZH2C784		
	Aug 1985	New to Hornsby, Ashby, Humberside as C51F			
	Sep 1985	Re-registered 7455 RH			
	Mar 1994	Toilet fitted becoming C49FT			
	Mar 1995	Hornsby allocated fleet number B13			
	Sep 2000	**Confidence, Leicester**			
	Jan 2007	Dismantled for spares and remains scrapped at Wigston depot			

No 43 was fitted with the more common type of Paramount 3500 body. Upon acquisition it ran in Hornsby livery, the pale blue being similar to the former grey livery of Confidence. It was very comfortable but the awkward, manual gearbox was not favoured by drivers which hastened its demise. The toilet was not used.

Above: **Seen arriving at its former home at Worth's of Enstone, during an enthusiasts' visit on 13 June 2009, is No 45 (B124 UUD) a Leyland Tiger with Plaxton Paramount II 3200 Express coachwork.**

Right: **The rear of No 45 showing the neat gold lettering and long 'Plaxtons' mud flap under the rear bumper.** Both: Simon Gill

45	B124 UUD	Leyland Tiger TRCTL11/3RH	8400388	C53F
		Plaxton Paramount II 3200 Express	8512LTP2X522	
	Dec 1984	New to City of Oxford Motor Services No 124 as C50F		
	Jul 1996	Worth, Enstone, Oxfordshire		
	Aug 1996	Re-seated to C53F		
	Apr 2001	**Confidence, Leicester**		
	Sep 2011	Wigley (dealer), Carlton, Barnsley for scrap		

This had the Mk II version of the body and differed from No 41, being fitted with the lower 3200 Express body which was more common elsewhere in the UK

50	A112 MUD	Leyland Tiger TRCTL11/3RH	8301148	C57F
		Plaxton Paramount 3200 Express	8412LTP1X536	
	Jan 1984	New to City of Oxford Motor Services No 112 as C51F		
	Jul 1996	Worth, Enstone, Oxfordshire as C57F		
	Jan 2002	**Confidence, Leicester**		
	Sep 2011	Wigley (dealer), Carlton, Barnsley for scrap		

No 50 differed from the other former City of Oxford 'City Link' express coaches, being fitted with the original version of the 3200 Express body.

56	B123 UUD	Leyland Tiger TRCTL11/3RH	8400384	C57F
		Plaxton Paramount II 3500 Express	8512LTP2X521	
	Dec 1984	New to City of Oxford Motor Services No 123 as C50F		
	Jul 1996	Worth, Enstone, Oxfordshire		
	Aug 1996	Re-seated to C57F		
	Aug 2002	**Confidence, Leicester**		
	Oct 2010	Dismantled for spares		
	Oct 2010	Remains to Wigston Car Breakers, Wigston for scrap		

The twin to No 45 purchased the year before which outlived No 56.

59	DCZ 2319	Leyland Tiger TRCTL11/2RH	8301004	C53F
		Plaxton Paramount 3200 Express	8411LTP1X534	
	Jan 1984	New to London Country Bus Services, Reigate No TP26 registered A126 EPA		
	Sep 1986	London Country North East, Hatfield No TP26		
	Jan 1989	Returned off lease to Kirby (dealer), Harthill, South Yorkshire		
	May 1989	Kentish Bus, Northfleet, Kent No 6		
	Jan 1990	Returned off lease to Kirby (dealer), Harthill, South Yorkshire		
	May 1990	Southend Transport No 564		
	Jul 1995	Lister (dealer), Bolton, Greater Manchester		
	Jul 1995	Thamesdown, Swindon, Wiltshire No 320		
	Mar 2000	Re-registered DCZ 2319 and renumbered 319 by Thamesdown		
	Apr 2003	**Confidence, Leicester**		
	Oct 2011	Cooper, Thetford, Norfolk for preservation re-registered A126 EPA		
	2014	Converted to a mobile home		

A large number of Leyland Tigers with Plaxton Paramount bodies were added to the London Country fleet to upgrade Green Line coach services in 1983/84. This one was new to Hertford garage to run services to the Guildford and north east London areas. When

The red front of No 50 (A112 MUD) gives it a different appearance to the Mk II body on No 45 with its smart silver finish. Note the sloping window line goes all the way to the front compared to the straight driver's window on No 45. Adrian Rodgers

The twin to No 45 where the Mk II frontal design allows space for a gold 'Confidence' fleet name which improves its appearance. Adrian Rodgers

London Country Bus Services was broken up, it passed to London Country North East on 7 September 1986 retaining the same fleet number. It moved to Grays garage in September 1987 before returning to a dealer in January 1989 upon expiry of the lease.

It was acquired by Kentish Bus for a short period and used at Dunton Green before ending up with Southend Transport where it stayed for five years. A move to Thamesdown saw it used on their country area services and, as noted above, it was re-registered and re-numbered. In September 2000, it was transferred to their 'Premier Training' driver training school before joining their schools fleet in January 2002.

Both Nos 59 & 60, at 11m long, were shorter than the other 12m Tigers in the fleet and were purchased as they were easier to manoeuvre around the back streets of Leicester. No 59 was re-registered and bought for preservation in 2011 but has since been converted for use as a mobile home where it was noted in use at the Glastonbury Festival in 2015.

60	DCZ 2317	Leyland Tiger TRCTL11/2RH	8301005	C53F
		Plaxton Paramount 3200 Express	8411LTP1X535	
	Jan 1984	New to London Country Bus Services, Reigate No TP27 registered A127 EPA		
	Sep 1986	London Country North East, Hatfield No TP27		
	Jan 1989	Returned off lease to Kirby (dealer), Harthill, South Yorkshire		
	Feb 1989	Maxfield, Sheffield, South Yorkshire		
	Mar 1989	Thamesdown, Swindon, Wiltshire No 317		
	Dec 1993	Named 'G J Churchward' by Thamesdown		
	Mar 2000	Re-registered DCZ 2317 by Thamesdown		
	Apr 2003	**Confidence, Leicester**		
	Dec 2016	Atkinson, Crewe for preservation		

This was another of the Leyland Tigers with Plaxton Paramount bodies added to the London Country fleet to upgrade Green Line coach services in 1984. It was also new to Hertford garage and ran the 930 service to Southend. When London Country Bus Services was broken up, it passed to London Country North East on 7 September 1986 retaining the same fleet number. Like No 59 it moved to Grays garage in September 1987 before returning to a dealer in January 1989 upon expiry of the lease.

It was tried by Maxfield, Sheffield for one month before passing to Thamesdown who named it 'G J Churchward' after the famous railway engineer. By May 2001 it had been transferred to their 'Premier Training' driver training school. After withdrawal by Confidence it was acquired for preservation.

Opposite page, top left: **With dirty side panels confirming its use on country area routes, Thamesdown No 320 (A126 EPA) is seen in Swindon bus station ready to operate the 48A service to Hungerford in the late 1990s.** Simon Gill Collection

Top right: **When No 59 (DCZ 2319) was acquired by Confidence it arrived in an all over white livery. It was outside Wigston depot on 7 June 2003.** Simon Gill

Bottom: **Leyland Tiger No 60 (DCZ 2317) is seen loading for a private hire excursion to Cheltenham on 31 May 2014.** Simon Gill

This page, top: **On 26 June 2004, No 59 shows off its red and black paintwork at Spalding Street depot.** Simon Gill

Below: **Fylde Borough Council No 27 (C27 ECW), the Leyland Tiger with Duple Laser coachwork, is seen when fairly new on the sea front at Blackpool on 29 September 1985.** Peter Cordwell

Below right: **Arriving at Uttoxeter Services on 12 June 2010 is No 62 (MJI 7846), by which time it was becoming a rare vehicle.** Simon Gill

62	MJI 7846	Leyland Tiger TRCTL11/3RH	8500071	C53F
		Duple Laser	8543/0638	
	Aug 1985	New to Fylde Borough Council, Lytham St Annes, Lancashire No 27 registered C27 ECW		
	Oct 1986	Transferred to Fylde Borough Transport Ltd, Lytham St Annes, Lancashire No 27		
	Jun 1990	Re-registered MJI 7846		
	Dec 1993	Transferred to Fylde Transport Ltd, Lytham St Anne's, Lancashire No 27		
	Jul 1996	Blackpool Transport Services, Blackpool, Lancashire No 27		
	Apr 1997	Paritrans (dealer), Cotes Heath, Staffordshire		
	Jun 1997	Martin Baker Aircraft Co, Higher Denham, Buckinghamshire as Non PSV		
	May 2004	**Confidence, Leicester**		
	Jan 2015	Wigley (dealer), Carlton, Barnsley for scrap		

No 62 was new to Fylde Borough Council in a pale blue livery with dark blue stripes. In the run up to deregulation the operation was incorporated and the fleet name 'Blue Buses' adopted, although it was still wholly owned by the Council. In December 1993 the operation was sold to a management buyout but independent ownership did not last long before selling out to Blackpool Transport in March 1994. The fleet was completely absorbed on 21 July 1996. It had been repainted into Seagull Coaches livery of two tone blue in February 1995.

In April 1997 it was sold to a dealer, passing to Martin Baker Aircraft Company, the ejection seat manufacturer, a few months later for staff transport.

When sold by Confidence it was the last Duple Laser bodied coach running in Leicestershire. It was a useful and popular member of the fleet.

Volvo B10M Coaches

With the Leyland Tiger no longer available it was necessary to look elsewhere and its successor, the Volvo B10M, was the obvious choice. The B10M replaced the Volvo B58 which had established Volvo in the British market. It did not appear in the UK until the Motor Show at the NEC, Birmingham in October 1980. The main difference was the B10M had an innovative jig welded chassis frame rather than the bolted frame of the B58, and offered full air suspension as standard.

Specification was similar to the B58 with a modified Volvo THD 100 9.6-litre engine making it more powerful and fuel efficient. The sales brochure at the time stated 'No other engine installation gives such perfect balance…and has such superior road-holding properties…' An updated B10M followed at the end of 1985 when Volvo announced a new generation THD101 engine, improved driver's area, redesigned electrics and improved lubrication, cooling and air systems. A further upgrade, the Mk III, came in 1989 with the THD102 engine giving 260 bhp and two radiators on the nearside – a conventional one and the other for an intercooler. The Volvo Easy Shift gearbox was also introduced.

A wide variety of coachwork was available, several of which have joined the Confidence fleet with many having been used on express services in various parts of the UK.

No 40 was the first vehicle in the fleet to have continental bodywork and also introduced the Midland Red inspired red and black coach livery. It had some well known owners over the years starting with Trathens, near Plymouth and then Graham, Paisley, Scotland. It was once used as a mobile film unit and then converted back to a fully seated coach which is fairly unusual.

On arrival it was extensively re-wired and for a short period it carried a Confidence Plus fleet name to promote its higher specification but this was soon deleted. The toilet was not used as there was nowhere to empty it!

This Volvo B10M with Van Hool body was new to the well known operator, Trathens of Yelverton near Plymouth. This rear view shows it was on contract to Top Deck Travel Holidays. The attractions in the rear window kept the passengers comfortable and entertained with a Video Show, Hi-fi stereo, Iced drinks, Hot drinks, Air suspension, Reclining seats, Air jet ventilation and Toilet. Paul Statham

Shortly after being acquired Confidence No 40 (BWT 199X) was attending an event at Saffron Lane Sports Stadium on 9 June 1999. It was in an all over red livery with no decals and was the first coach painted in the new red and black coach livery. Adrian Rodgers

The black trim was a great improvement to the look of No 40 which was on a private hire when seen at Beaumanor Hall, Leicestershire on 21 May 2010. Adrian Rodgers

40	BWT 199X	Volvo B10M-61		YV3B10M610000889	C48FT
		Van Hool T8 Alizee		9934	
	Sep 1981	New to Trathens, Yelverton, Devon, registered STT 611X as C49FT			
	Sep 1983	Graham, Paisley, Renfrewshire, No S7			
	Apr 1994	Re-registered 735 JVO			
	May 1990	Haldane, Glasgow, Strathclyde			
	Jan 1992	Converted to C20FT as a mobile film unit by this date			
	Mar 1995	Bennett, Warrington, Cheshire			
	Nov 1995	Converted to C48FT by Bennett, Warrington			
	Jun 1996	Hudson, Bilborough, North Yorkshire			
	Jun 1997	La Pilusa and Simpson, Copmanthorpe, North Yorkshire			
	Dec 1998	Plaxton (dealer), Anston, South Yorkshire by this date – re-registered BWT 199X			
	Mar 1999	**Confidence, Leicester**			
	Oct 2011	Re-registered DCZ 2319 from no 59 (A126 EPA)			
	May 2014	Ripley (dealer), Carlton, Barnsley for scrap			

The second of the two Volvo B10Ms that introduced the Plaxton Premier Interurban coach to Scottish express services, alongside K561 GSA, was No 570 (K570 GSA). Allocated to Stagecoach Scotland, it is seen loading in Perth on 7 September 1995, a very wet day. Simon Gill

64	K561 GSA	Volvo B10M-60	YV31MGC19PA030738	C51F
		Plaxton Premier Interurban	9212VCM0808	
	Feb 1993	New to Stagecoach Scotland, Perth, No 561 registered K561 GSA and seating C53F		
	Oct 1994	Bluebird Buses, Aberdeen, Grampian, No 561 as C51F		
	Dec 1999	Re-registered TSV 718		
	Jan 2003	Re-numbered 52131 by Bluebird Buses		
	Dec 2004	Re-registered back to K561 GSA		
	Jun 2005	**Confidence, Leicester**		
	Sep 2016	Scrapped		

Right: **After arrival at Confidence, No 64 (K561 KSA) received the red and black coach livery. It is seen at Stonehurst Farm Park, Mountsorrel on 22 June 2009.** Adrian Rodgers

Far right: **Five years later on 25 June 2014 and parked in exactly the same location is No 64 (K561 KSA). It had been repainted in a more contemporary all over silver grey livery but retaining the black roof.** Adrian Rodgers

The Plaxton Premier Interurban was introduced by Stagecoach in 1993 on a network of limited stop express services in northeast Scotland. The Plaxton body was a simplified version of their standard Premier 320 coach with fixed seats and bus type features, such as the destination gear.

As Stagecoach No 561 this was, numerically, the first one of two allocated to their 'head office' Stagecoach Scotland fleet in Perth where it was given a 'Perth Panther' fleet name. It moved to Bluebird Buses the following year where it joined No 66 (K562 GSA). The 'Stagecoach Express' branded services became extremely popular with the frequency of the Aberdeen to Inverness service being increased to half-hourly to meet demand.

After twelve arduous years in Scotland No 64 joined Confidence where it gave another eleven years' service before being scrapped in 2016.

66	K562 GSA	Volvo B10M-60		YV31MGC14PA030744	C51F
		Plaxton Premier Interurban		9212VCM0814	
	Feb 1993	New to Bluebird Buses, Aberdeen, Grampian, No 562 registered K562 GSA and seating C53F			
	Aug 1993	Re-seated to C51F			
	Dec 1999	Re-registered TSV 719			
	Jan 2003	Re-numbered 52132			
	Dec 2004	Re-registered back to K562 GSA			
	Apr 2005	Mallinson, Stocksbridge, South Yorkshire			
	Feb 2006	Plaxton (dealer), Anston, South Yorkshire			
	Feb 2006	**Confidence, Leicester**			
	Sep 2017	Dismantled for spares and remains scrapped at the Wigston depot			

No 66 has a similar history to No 64. It operated for Stagecoach's Bluebird Buses' subsidiary from garages, including Macduff, Elgin, Peterhead, Perth and Inverness where it finished before sale.

68	L151 HUD	Volvo B10M-62		YV31M2B11RA040199	C55F
		Plaxton Premier 350		9412VUP1565	
	Dec 1993	City of Oxford Motor Services, Oxford, No 151 seating C53F			
	Mar 2001	Worth, Enstone, Oxfordshire			
	Feb 2007	**Confidence, Leicester**			
	Aug 2019	Dismantled for spares			
	Aug 2019	Remains to Wigston Car Breakers, Wigston for scrap			

The history of No 68 is almost the same as the Leyland Tiger's in that it spent its time with City of Oxford on the X90 'City Link' express services between Oxford, London and Heathrow Airport. It then passed to Worth's of Enstone from whom Confidence bought it in 2007. It operated in Worth's livery with Confidence fleet names applied.

73	L154 HUD	Volvo B10M-62		YV31M2B18RA040202	C55F
		Plaxton Premier 350		9412VUP1568	
	Dec 1993	City of Oxford Motor Services, Oxford No 154 seating C53F			
	Mar 2001	Worth, Enstone, Oxfordshire			
	Nov 2011	**Confidence, Leicester**			
	Still in use				

No 73 is another former City of Oxford coach to arrive via Worth's of Enstone. It carries an all over light grey livery and remains in use at the time of writing.

80	L671 OHL	Volvo B10M-62		YV31M2B11RA040705	C70F
		Plaxton Premier 320		9412VUM2499	
	Apr 1994	New to Fleet Coaches, Fleet, Hampshire, No L1, registered L671 OHL, seating C53F			
	Jun 2001	Coach Europe (dealer), Ratby, Leicestershire			
	Jul 2001	Pulham, Bourton-on-the-Water, Gloucestershire			
	Jan 2002	Re-registered XDG 614			
	Aug 2013	Re-seated to C70F for school work			
	Apr 2015	Re-registered L15 PUL			
	Jan 2016	Re-registered back to L671 OHL			
	Apr 2016	**Confidence, Leicester**			
	Still in use				

No 80 was new to Fleet Coaches, Hampshire as L671 OHL in April 1994. It passed to the well known operator Pulham's to operate a variety of coach work in Bourton-on-the-Water, which is known as the 'Venice of the Cotswolds'. In 2013 it was re-seated with '3+2' seating to increase its capacity for school work, passing to Confidence in this configuration – the highest seating capacity of any Confidence coach. It is in a different livery of red and grey having had Pulham's cream over-painted in grey.

Opposite, top: **On 14 March 2006 the second Volvo B10M/Plaxton Premier Interurban, No 66 (K562 KSA), was photographed at Enderby in this white and blue livery, applied during its brief time with Mallinson.** Adrian Rodgers

Bottom left: **Soon repainted into the red and black livery No 66 looked the same as its twin No 64.** Trevor Follows

Bottom right: **Unlike No 64, No 66 was never repainted into the silver/grey livery and was broken up for spares at Wigston depot when its service life ended.** Simon Gill Collection

This page, top left: **No 68 (L151 HUD), a B10M with a high floor Plaxton Premier 350 body is a former City of Oxford express coach but, unlike the Paramount 3500 Express bodied Tigers, it had a coach type door. It is seen at Beaumanor Hall, Leicestershire on 10 June 2014.** Adrian Rodgers

Top right: **The second former City of Oxford Volvo B10M, No 73 (L154 HUD) was repainted into the 'new' all over silver grey coach livery and is seen at Stonehurst Farm Park, Mountsorrel on 3 July 2012. A popular destination for school trips.** Adrian Rodgers

Centre: **A change of livery where Pulham's cream has been repainted grey sees No 80 (L671 OHL) in this attractive red, grey and black scheme with large 'Confidence' fleet name. It is the only coach to seat 70 passengers with three seats on one side of the coach and two on the other side. Ideal for school work. It was seen attending a rally at Quorn and Woodhouse station on 22 April 2017.** Simon Gill

Bottom: **No 80 looks just as attractive from the rear and belies its 26 years on the road.** Simon Gill

89	T325 LAF	Volvo B10M-62	YV31MA611XC061138	C53F
		Berkhof Axial 50	3887	
	May 1999	New to Hodge, Sandhurst, Berkshire registered 8896 PH, as C51FT		
	Dec 2008	McCree (dealer), Shepshed, Leicestershire and re-registered T325 LAF		
	Jan 2001	Leggs (T/A Mitcham Belle), Raynes Park, London		
	Oct 2018	Confidence, Leicester		
	Oct 2018	Toilet removed and changed to C53F		
		Still in use		

No 89 is the latest coach to be acquired and only the second one to have a continental body.

The Berkhof name disappeared in 2010 following a takeover by the VDL Group in 1998.

New as 8896 PH it was re-registered T325 LAF, in December 2008, when acquired by Leggs trading as 'Mitcham Belle'. It remains in Legg's livery with their fleet name replaced by a 'Travel with Confidence' fleet name.

On acquisition as C51FT, the toilet was removed and two seats added to make it C53F.

The smart interior of No 89 includes mostly blue moquette seats, with seat belts, and red curtains.

The latest fleet name encourages passengers to 'Travel with Confidence.

No 89 (T325 LAF) is the latest Volvo B10M coach to join the fleet and only the second with a continental body – this time built by Berkhof of the Netherlands. It retains its last operator's livery and has had the fleet name changed to an attractive 'Travel with Confidence' logo. A new 'Club Class' dawns. All: Simon Gill

Volvo Citybus

The Volvo Citybus was a variation of the mid-engined B10M with lowered suspension to make it suitable for double deck bodywork. It was initially built at Volvo's Irvine factory from 1982; production moving to Boras, Sweden in 1986. Even with lower suspension the under-floor engine resulted in the finished bus being higher than conventional double-deckers, the main benefit being a completely flat lower saloon floor with an enhanced seating capacity as there was no rear engine. Production peaked in 1989/90 and the model was phased out when Volvo bought Leyland and concentrated on the Olympian.

The largest order for the Citybus in 1988, worth £2.5m, was from Grey Green whose successful tender to operate London Regional Transport route 24 from Hampstead Heath to Pimlico was announced in April 1988. This required 30 of the type and deliveries began on 12 September in good time for the start on 5 November 1988. The smart grey, green and orange buses made a good impression, especially as they passed the Houses of Parliament, 10 Downing Street and London Transport's 55 Broadway headquarters. With coach rated 245bhp engines they were the most powerful buses in service in the UK. They were sold in 2003.

Grey Green 127 (F127 PHM), the Volvo Citybus B10M-50 with Alexander dual door body, is seen in Charing Cross Road on 9 May 1994 operating route 24 to Hampstead Heath. Simon Gill Collection

74	F127 PHM	Volvo Citybus B10M-50	YV31MGC19JA018774	H46/40F
		Alexander RV-type	RV35/2188/13	
	Oct 1988	New to Cowie (T/A Grey Green), Stamford Hill, London, No 127 seating H45/29D		
	Sep 1999	Arriva London North East, Barking, London, No 127		
	Apr 2002	Re-numbered VA127 by Arriva London North East		
	Aug 2003	Fleetlink (dealer), Mossley Hill, Liverpool		
	Jan 2004	Locallink Buses, Great Dunmow & Stanstead, Essex		
	Apr 2004	Southdown PSV (dealer), Copthorne, East Surrey		
	Jul 2004	Loaned to Surrey Connect, Gatwick, West Sussex		
	Aug 2004	Marshalls, Sutton-on-Trent, Nottinghamshire, No DD68		
	Oct 2009	Converted to H46/40F by Marshalls, Sutton-on-Trent		
	Oct 2012	Confidence, Leicester		
	Oct 2018	Withdrawn		
	Oct 2019	Ripley (dealer), Carlton, Barnsley		

Marshalls of Sutton-on-Trent operated F127 PHM as their No DD68 between 2004 and 2012. It is seen at East Muskham, Nottinghamshire in April 2011 with similar DD69 (H3 YRR) which was new to Burnley & Pendle as No 114 (H114 ABV) in January 1991. Trevor Follows

Confidence 74 was operating a private hire when photographed on 14 June 2018. Its extra height can easily be appreciated compared to Leyland Olympian/ECW No 61 (CUD 221Y) parked alongside. Adrian Rodgers

All 30 Citybuses were allocated to Stamford Hill garage. No 74 was one of seven repainted overall deep red in 1997 to operate a Bakerloo tube replacement service between Oxford Circus and Elephant & Castle. October 1997 saw the Cowie Group re-named Arriva plc and the name started to replace Grey Green on the buses from January 1998. There was little immediate change to those operating route 24 but eventually it was repainted, in May 1998, in London red with Arriva style white/cream horns.

After sale in 2003 No 74 moved around the UK during 2004 before settling at Marshalls who converted it to single door by October 2009. It was withdrawn by Confidence in October 2018, mainly due to being non-standard and care being required as to where it could be used. It was kept in reserve for 12 months before sale in case it was needed, being sold to Ripley as a runner and driven away.

Dennis Trident

The low floor Dennis Trident was unveiled in 1997 and Stagecoach became a major customer, switching from its traditional supplier, Volvo. The London specification was 10.5m long and included a transverse 8.3 litre, 220bhp Cummins C-series Euro 2 engine coupled to a Voith DIWA gearbox. The dual door Alexander body seated 71 passengers, although there were severe constraints on the lower deck given the need to accommodate two doors and space for wheelchairs and buggies.

By the end of 1999 Stagecoach in London had 200 in service, or on order, having started the year with none. After a mere ten years' service in London Confidence was able to snap up this relatively young double decker. Since then it has not been without its challenges but remains an active member of the fleet.

So, hot on the heels of the first new bus, No 71, came this Dennis Trident which has also remained unique in the fleet. Whilst in London it operated from Plumstead garage until August 2009 when it spent its final two months at Catford garage. The apparent change of operator was due to Stagecoach selling its London

Top: **The Dennis Trident with Alexander ALX400 body, No 72 (V125 MEV) entered service in Selkent all over red livery, still carrying fleet number 17125. It was photographed on 14 April 2010.** Adrian Rodgers

Below: **Just reversed off the pit at Wigston garage on 28 August 2019 is No 72 which has now been in the fleet for over 10 years.** Simon Gill

operations to the East London Bus Group (Macquarie Bank). It was converted to single door layout by Ensign prior to acquisition and initially ran in all over London red before being repainted.

72	V125 MEV	Dennis Trident 2		SFD311BR1XGX20629	H47/31F
		Alexander ALX400		9915/27	
	Nov 1999	New to Stagecoach Selkent, West Ham, No TA125 seating H47/24D			
	Jan 2003	Re-numbered 17125 by Stagecoach Selkent			
	Aug 2006	East London Bus Group, West Ham, No 17125			
	Oct 2009	Ensign (dealer), Purfleet, Essex and converted to H47/31F			
	Dec 2009	**Confidence, Leicester**			
		Still in use			

Volvo Olympians

When Volvo acquired Leyland, the only double deck chassis they produced was the high floor Citybus. With the announcement that the Leyland factory was to close they quickly followed this up with news that production of the world's best selling double-decker, the Olympian, would continue at their Irvine factory – Volvo appreciated the value of the lower floored chassis and, above all, wanted to retain customer loyalty.

Modifications were made to the specification with Volvo's 9.6 litre TD102KF engine offered in addition to Cummins, which had been an option in later Leyland built chassis. About 60% of the mechanical units were changed to Volvo and the B10M instrument binnacle was added for drivers. It was the first time Volvo had offered a chassis with a transverse mounted engine. The Volvo engine was modified to comply with Euro 2 emissions in 1996, at which time the Cummins option was dropped as their new unit was too large to fit in the engine bay. New legislation, requiring all forms of transport to have disabled access, saw the introduction of low floor double-deckers in 1998 and interest in the Olympian slumped; the last ones for the UK and Ireland leaving the factory in summer 2000, twenty years after the first prototypes had been unveiled.

Dublin Bus remained a loyal customer of the Olympian, mostly with locally built Alexander (Belfast) bodies, buying 640 of the type.

It had the distinction of placing the last Olympian, No RV630 (99 D 630), into service in October 2000 although it was not the last one built. As can be seen below, these have proved popular with Confidence in recent years and Nos 83 and 84 were amongst the last ones built.

No 79 was delivered to Dublin Bus in their blue/cream/orange livery, spending time at their Donnybrook, Harristown and Summerhill garages. It spent 18 months in Oxfordshire before moving to Confidence where the conversion to single door was completed and it was repainted in Confidence livery.

To show the livery that was carried by some of the Volvo Olympians when they entered service in Dublin here is Dublin Bus RV533 (99 D 533) on 25 June 2002. Simon Gill

79	T308 YAW	Volvo Olympian OLY-50	YV3YNA41XXC029657	H47/34F
		Alexander (Belfast) RH-type	9901/02	
	Aug 1999	New to Dublin Bus, Dublin, No RV557 registered 99 D 557 and seating H47/27D		
	Oct 2012	Withdrawn by Dublin Bus		
	Mar 2013	Drew Wilson (dealer), Carluke, Ireland		
	Sep 2013	School Bus Company, Kingston Bagpuize, Oxfordshire, No 67 re-registered T308 YAW		
	Apr 2015	Confidence, Leicester		
	Apr 2015	Converted to H47/34F by Confidence		
		Still in use		

The Olympians were repainted into this blue and yellow livery with white trim. No RV557 (99 D 557) joined the Confidence fleet as No 79, re-registered T308 YAW. It was seen in Dublin on 16 April 2011. Simon Gill

The next time the writer saw RV557 was on 28 August 2019 as Confidence No 79 (T308 YAW). It was parked awaiting its next trip. Simon Gill

81	T479 KDM	Volvo Olympian OLY-50	YV3YNA415XC029551	H47/27D
	Alexander (Belfast) RH-type	9829/37		
	Mar 1999	New to Dublin Bus, Dublin, No RV482, registered 99 D 482		
	Apr 2009	Withdrawn		
	Feb 2010	Al's Coaches, Birkenhead, Merseyside		
	Apr 2010	Re-registered T479 KDM		
	Aug 2016	Confidence, Leicester		
		Still in use		

Delivered to Dublin Bus in their blue/cream/orange livery, it spent its life at their Donnybrook garage before purchase by Happy Al's, Birkenhead. This was one of four Olympians bought from Al's to operate a new contract to Countesthorpe College. They were all collected on 24 August 2016 from Birkenhead. Repainted in Confidence livery.

82	V311 JMB	Volvo Olympian OLY-50	YV3YNA413XC029712	H47/31F
	Alexander (Belfast) RH-type	9901/57		
	Dec 1999	New to Dublin Bus, Dublin, No RV612, registered 99 D 612 and seating H47/27D		
	Aug 2010	Al's Coaches, Birkenhead, Merseyside		
	Oct 2010	Re-registered V311 JMB		
	Aug 2016	Confidence, Leicester		
	Dec 2016	Converted to H47/31F by Confidence		
		Still in use		

Delivered to Dublin Bus in their City Swift livery, it spent time at their Coyningham Road and Phibsborough garages before passing to Happy Al's, Birkenhead. Collected on Wednesday 24 August 2016, the middle doors were removed, four extra seats added and it was fully repainted by December 2016.

Confidence No 81 (T479 KDM) had been repainted in fleet livery when photographed on 30 October 2017. Adrian Rodgers

83	V363 JMB	Volvo Olympian OLY-50	YV3YNA414XC029718	H47/27D
		Alexander (Belfast) RH-type	9901/63	
	Dec 1999	New to Dublin Bus, Dublin, No RV618, registered 99 D 618		
	Jul 2011	Al's Coaches, Birkenhead, Merseyside		
	Nov 2011	Re-registered V363 JMB		
	Aug 2016	Confidence, Leicester		
		Still in use		

One of the last Olympians built, No 83 was delivered to Dublin Bus in their City Swift livery spending time at their Coyningham Road and Harristown garages before passing to Happy Al's, Birkenhead. It was collected on Wednesday 24 August 2016 and has been repainted in Confidence livery.

Representing the attractive City Swift livery that three of the buses were delivered in is similar Dublin Bus RV569 (99 D 569). It was seen near Dublin railway station on 25 June 2002. Simon Gill

No 82 (V311 JMB) was converted to single door on arrival at Confidence and repainted. It was photographed on 22 June 2018. Adrian Rodgers

Above: **On 18 June 2018 No 83 (V363 JMB), one of the last Olympians to be built, was seen on Scudamore Road, Leicester. At that stage, fleet names had not been applied.** Adrian Rodgers

Below: **At the time of writing, one of the ex-Dublin Volvo Olympians, No 84 (V364 JMB) remains in this blue and yellow livery. It was photographed on 11 December 2018.** Adrian Rodgers

84	V364 JMB	Volvo Olympian OLY-50	YV3YNA412XC029717	H47/27D
		Alexander (Belfast) RH-type	9901/62	
	Dec 1999	New to Dublin Bus, Dublin, No RV617, registered 99 D 617		
	Jul 2011	Al's Coaches, Birkenhead, Merseyside		
	Nov 2011	Re-registered V364 JMB		
	Aug 2016	Confidence, Leicester		
		Still in use		

One of the last Olympians built, No 84 was delivered to Dublin Bus in their City Swift livery spending time at their Coyningham Road and Harristown garages before passing to Happy Al's, Birkenhead. It was collected on Wednesday 24 August 2016 and remains in the last Dublin livery of yellow and blue pending repainting.

90	T478 KDM	Volvo Olympian OLY-50	YV3YNA419XC029553	H47/31F
		Alexander (Belfast) RH-type	9829/39	
	Mar 1999	New to Dublin Bus, Dublin, No RV484, registered 99 D 484 and seating H47/27D		
	May 2009	Withdrawn		
	Feb 2010	Al's Coaches, Birkenhead, Merseyside		
	Apr 2010	Re-registered T478 KDM and re-seated to H47/31F		
	Oct 2015	Dixon, Leicester, Leicestershire		
	Apr 2019	Confidence, Leicester		
	Jun 2019	Entered service after refurbishment and repainting.		
		Still in use		

This was how T478 KDM appeared when owned by Dixon, Leicester on 27 October 2015 and it was the same when acquired by Confidence in April 2019. Adrian Rodgers

The latest arrival in the fleet is No 90 (T478 KDM). After some hard work it looks far better than it did in the previous photograph. Simon Gill

Delivered to Dublin Bus in their blue/cream/orange livery it spent its life at their Donnybrook garage before purchase by Happy Al's, Birkenhead. Sold to Dixons of Leicester. This latest addition to the fleet was acquired in a relatively poor condition so was refurbished and repainted over the following few months; entering service on Monday 10 June 2019.

DAF DB250

The DB250LF was the first low floor double-deck chassis available in the UK, being introduced at the beginning of 1998 with Optare Spectra bodywork. Arriva London soon ordered some with Alexander ALX400 bodies and both Nos 85 and 86 were among the very first new generation, fully accessible, low floor double-deckers to enter service in London in November 1998 on route 242 between Tottenham Court Road and Homerton Hospital. They were part of the first batch of 64 buses (Arriva London North Nos DLA1 – 64) and operated from Clapton garage. When new the buses received a lot of publicity.

When withdrawn they were the oldest low floor double-deckers in service in London lasting nearly 14 years – latterly on route W3 between Finsbury Park Station – Alexandra Palace – Northumberland Park Station. The buses were then cascaded to Arriva's provincial fleets and both ended up in the West Midlands before being acquired by Confidence.

85	S213 JUA	DAF DE02RSDB250		XMGDE02RS0H006954	H45/23F
		Alexander ALX400		9724/12	
	Nov 1998	New to Arriva London North, Wood Green, London, No DLA13 seating H45/17D			
	Jan 2002	Re-seated to H45/21D			
	Sep 2007	Re-seated to H45/19D			
	Feb 2012	Withdrawn & transferred to Arriva, Derby for conversion to single door			
	Oct 2012	Arriva Midlands North, Cannock No 4787 converted to H45/23F			
	Nov 2016	Confidence, Leicester			
		Still in use			

No 85 was originally allocated to Clapton garage before moving to Wood Green in May 2006. It transferred to Lea Valley garage in September 2011 before withdrawal in February 2012.

Conversion to single door was undertaken at Arriva, Derby before it entered service with Arriva Midlands North, No 4787, at Telford garage in October 2012. In November 2014 it was transferred to Wednesfield garage, moving back to Telford in January 2015, before being withdrawn in September 2016. It was again taken to Arriva, Derby who repainted it into Confidence black and grey livery before collection as part of the sale agreement.

86	S214 JUA	DAF DE02RSDB250		XMGDE02RS0H006957	H45/21F
		Alexander ALX400		9724/13	
	Nov 1998	New to Arriva London North, Wood Green, London, No DLA14 seating H45/17D			
	Jan 2002	Re-seated to H45/21D			
	Oct 2007	Re-seated to H45/19D			
	Feb 2012	Withdrawn & transferred to Arriva, Derby for conversion to single door			
	Aug 2012	Arriva Midlands North, Cannock No 4788 converted to H45/21F			
	Nov 2016	**Confidence, Leicester**			
		Not in use but still owned			

Opposite page, top: **Seen shortly after collection on a damp 11 December 2016 is Alexander ALX400-bodied DAF DB250 No 85 (S213 JUA). It was still devoid of fleet names and numbers.** Adrian Rodgers

Bottom: **A very smart No 85 at Wigston depot on 28 August 2019 with dot-matrix destination indicator all set for the next school service.** Simon Gill

This page, top left: **On 28 July 2015, S214 JUA was working as Arriva Midlands North No 4788 at Oswestry in the 'local landmarks' livery. The offside was in English.** Simon Gill

Top right: **The Welsh language featured on the nearside as No 4788 shows in Oswestry bus station.** Simon Gill

Bottom: **No 86 (S214 SUA) was parked at Wigston depot on 6 December 2017 with nowhere to go. Still devoid of fleet names and numbers it has been used to provide spares for No 85.** Adrian Rodgers

No 86 was originally allocated to Clapton garage before moving to Wood Green in May 2006. A further transfer to Lea Valley occurred in September 2011 before withdrawal the following February.

Conversion to single door was undertaken at Arriva, Derby before it entered service with Arriva Midlands North, No 4788, at Oswestry garage in August 2012. It was operated there on Oswestry shopper and school bus routes 403/405 in a 'local landmarks' livery created by local artist, 'The Artful Jotter'.

Withdrawn in September 2016, it was again taken to Arriva, Derby who painted it into Confidence black and grey livery before collection. Sadly, it has never been used so fleet names have not been applied. It has been used for spares to keep No 85 on the road.

Volvo B7TLs

The Volvo B7TL was the low floor replacement for the Olympian but Volvo was slow to bring it to the market, having failed to gain orders for their proposed 36ft (11m) B7L chassis, which gave Dennis a significant three year advantage. The shorter B7TL, with a conventional transverse rear engine, finally appeared in 2000 with Go-Ahead Group subsidiary, London Central, one of the lead operators. The first batch was numbered AVL1 – 46 and three of these are currently in the Confidence fleet. At that time, Transdev subsidiary, London United, also bought a batch of 45 similar examples (Nos VA60 – 104) and two of these are also operated.

As with the sole Dennis Trident and DAF DB250s, bodywork is the popular Alexander ALX400. Production of the B7TL ended in 2006 when it fell foul of new noise emission regulations in London.

75	V110 LGC	Volvo B7TL	YV3S2C613YC000106	H43/27F
		Alexander ALX400	9833/10	
	Jan 2000	New to London Central, Merton, No AVL10 as H43/20D		
	Jun 2007	Re-seated to H43/17D		
	May 2009	Blue Triangle, Rainham, No AVL10		
	Jul 2009	Southdown PSV (dealer), Copthorne, West Sussex		
	Nov 2012	**Confidence, Leicester**		
	Dec 2012	Converted to H43/27F		
		Still in use		

New to Peckham garage for route 63 (Kings Cross – Crystal Palace), No 75 was transferred to Camberwell garage in June 2006, being down-seated to H43/17D by the removal of 3 tip-up seats. In May 2009 it was transferred from Camberwell to the associated Blue Triangle fleet at Rainham. It was withdrawn in July 2009 and returned off lease to Volvo and moved to Southdown PSV for re-sale. It spent over three years at the dealer before being sold to Confidence.

No 75 initially ran in all over white livery with underlined Confidence fleet name below the front upper deck windows (above the driver's window and the door) and was then gradually repainted as time allowed.

The first Volvo B7TL to join the fleet, No 75 (V110 LGC), entered service in all over white with black 'Confidence' fleet names and numbers and remained so for some time. It was seen at Beaumanor Hall on 2 July 2014.

No 75 was gradually repainted as time allowed and by 21 May 2015, the lower panels were black with white fleet numbers.

By 15 September 2015, No 75 was in full fleet livery with a white fleet name positioned in the usual places on the lower panels. In this view it is seen just off Saffron Lane – the driver will need to take care of the overhanging tree branches when he leaves. All: Adrian Rodgers

77	V188 OOE	Volvo B7TL	YV3S2C615YC000222	H43/27F
		Alexander ALX400	9940/13	
	Feb 2000	New to London United, Twickenham, No VA72 as H43/20D		
	Nov 2010	Withdrawn and stored		
	Feb 2011	Reinstated by London United.		
	Mar 2011	Ownership changed from Transdev to RATP-Dev.		
	Feb 2013	Withdrawn by London United		
	May 2014	Ripley (dealer), Carlton, Barnsley by this date		
	May 2014	**Confidence, Leicester**		
	May 2014	Converted to H43/27F by Confidence		
		Still in use		

New as London United VA72, it was allocated to Shepherds Bush garage. In November 2010 it was withdrawn and transferred to Hounslow Heath garage for storage before being reinstated at Hounslow in February 2011. Transdev sold London United to RATP-Dev the following month and, in September 2012, it was transferred to Fulwell garage before being withdrawn in February 2013. By May 2014 it had been sold to Ripley (dealer) who sold it to Confidence where it was converted to single door.

Confidence No 77 (V188 OOE) was parked in Harrison Close on 28 August 2019. Unlike the others it has yellow school bus logos on either side of the destination glass. Simon Gill

No 78 (V208 OOE) is another smart member of this class of low floor double-deckers, its panels glistening in the summer sunshine at Wigston depot on 28 August 2019. Simon Gill

78	V208 OOE	Volvo B7TL	YV3S2C619YC000210	H43/27F
		Alexander ALX400	9955/7	
	Mar 2000	New to London United, Twickenham, No VA85 as H43/20D		
	Mar 2011	Ownership changed from Transdev to RATP-Dev.		
	Jun 2013	Withdrawn by London United		
	Mar 2014	Ripley (dealer), Carlton, Barnsley by this date		
	Mar 2014	**Confidence, Leicester**		
		Converted to H43/27F by Confidence – Still in use		

New as London United VA85, it was allocated to Shepherds Bush garage. In October 2010 it was transferred to Hounslow garage. Transdev sold London United to RATP-Dev on 3 March 2011. In September 2012 it was transferred back to Shepherds Bush garage before moving for the last time to Fulwell garage in January 2013. It was withdrawn in June 2013. By March 2014 it had been sold to Ripley (dealer) who sold it to Confidence where it was converted to single door.

Still in the livery of Luckett's of Fareham on 15 February 2019 is No 87 (V132 LGC). It will be repainted as soon as time allows. Adrian Rodgers

87	V132 LGC	Volvo B7TL		YV3S2C612YC000159	H47/27F
		Alexander ALX400	9833/32		
	Jan 2000	New to London Central, Merton, No AVL32 as H43/20D			
	Dec 2005	Re-seated to H43/17D			
	Dec 2009	Withdrawn			
	Jul 2012	Luckett, Fareham, Hampshire, No 7404 converted to H47/27F			
	Oct 2012	Re-registered A4 SDL by Luckett, Fareham			
	Jun 2014	Re-numbered 740474 by Luckett, Fareham			
	Oct 2017	Re-registered back to V132 LGC by Luckett, Fareham			
	Nov 2017	**Confidence, Leicester**			
		Still in use			

Like No 75, this Volvo was allocated to Peckham garage for route 63 when it was new and was down-seated to H43/17D in December 2005 by removal of 3 tip-up seats. It was withdrawn in December 2009 and placed in storage, being returned off lease to Volvo the following month. It was sold to Luckett, Fareham and converted to single door with seat belts, before passing to Confidence where it is currently in use in Luckett's livery.

88	V144 LGC	Volvo B7TL		YV3S2C61XYC000183	H47/27F
		Alexander ALX400	9833/44		
	Feb 2000	New to London Central, Merton, No AVL44 as H43/20D			
	Aug 2008	Re-seated to H43/17D			
	Dec 2009	Withdrawn			
	Jul 2012	Luckett, Fareham, Hampshire, No 7405 converted to H47/27F			
	Oct 2012	Re-registered A10 HLC by Luckett, Fareham			
	Jun 2014	Re-numbered 740574 by Luckett, Fareham			
	Oct 2017	Re-registered back to V144 LGC by Luckett, Fareham			
	Nov 2017	**Confidence, Leicester**			
		Still in use			

Like No 87, this Volvo was allocated to Peckham garage for route 63 when it was new and was down-seated to H43/17D in August 2008 by removal of 3 tip-up seats. It was withdrawn in December 2009 and placed in storage, being returned off lease to Volvo the following month. It was sold to Luckett, Fareham and converted to single door with seat belts, before passing to Confidence where it is currently in use in Luckett's livery.

Parked on Green Lane Road, Leicester awaiting its next duty on 28 August 2019 is No 88 (V144 LGC). This also retains Luckett's grey livery for the time being as it is not too dissimilar to Confidence. Simon Gill

The New Volvo B9TL

The only new bus ever acquired by Confidence was this Volvo B9TL. The B9TL first appeared in 2005 to replace the B7TL which had been introduced in a hurry and, although some modifications were made, it needed an upgrade. The B9TL featured a new Volvo D9B engine. Initially the chassis was only offered with a Wright body but this was later changed so other manufacturers could also supply bodywork.

Negotiations to buy the complete bus started with Darwen East Lancs in early 2008. The former East Lancashire Coachbuilders had gone into administration on 17 August 2007 but was saved and bought by the Darwen Group the next day, being re-branded Darwen East Lancs. An order was placed for their Olympus body which had been introduced in 2006.

In the meantime, Optare had been acquired by the Chairman of the Darwen Group, Ron Stanley, through a company called Jamesstan Investments in which he had a controlling interest. Optare initially remained separate but on 17 July 2008 a reverse takeover by the Darwen Group was completed and Optare PLC was formed. This merged the Optare factory in Leeds with the former East Lancs factory at Blackburn and the Optare name was adopted. This is why No 71 was ordered as an East Lancs/Darwen Olympus but ended up as an Optare Olympus.

No 71 arrived in December 2008. The smart 10.9m low height bus was fitted with 74 Abacus Bodyguard 2000 high backed seats plus three fold down seats in the lower saloon. The high backed seats gave better comfort and more leg room than if they had gone for a higher seating capacity.

Ventilation was provided by a Grayson blown and standard convection heating system with gasket mounted side windows. A manual destination blind was fitted. The bus was a strong statement about the future.

The loss of the bus, due to an electrical fire, in June 2018 not only destroyed the engine compartment but damage to electrical circuits meant repair was not possible. It was a sad end to a nicely appointed vehicle.

Looking magnificent in the sunshine at Wollaton Park, Nottingham on 31 May 2009 is No 71 (FJ58 CON). The sleek low height and high backed seats will be noted. Simon Gill

The fire takes hold in the engine compartment of No 71 in late June 2018. Ken Williams Collection

71	FJ58 CON	Volvo B9TL	YV3S4L8249A130568	DPH47/30F
		Optare Olympus	70301	
	Dec 2008	New to Confidence, Leicester		
	Jun 2018	Severely damaged by an electrical fire		
	Jul 2018	Lloyd (dealer), Hixon, Staffordshire for scrap		

KENNETH M WILLIAMS T/A CONFIDENCE COACHES AND CONFIDENCE BUS & COACH HIRE LTD – FLEET SUMMARY AS OF MARCH 2020

No	Registration	Chassis	Body	Seating	New	Acquired	Date Out
1	PUF 647	Guy Arab IV (6LW)	Park Royal	H33/26RD	May-56	May-70	Mar-74
2	LDB 779	AEC Reliance 2MU3RA	Harrington Wayfarer IV	C41F	Mar-59	Nov-71	Feb-73
3	456 FUP	Bedford SB1	Duple Super Vega	C41F	Jan-60	Jan-73	May-75
4	XUF 845	Leyland Titan PD3/4	Northern Counties	FH39/30F	Nov-59	Aug-73	Sep-80
5	749 DCD	Leyland Leopard L2	Harrington Grenadier	C39F	Oct-63	Mar-75	Jan-86
6	LRU 72	Bristol Lodekka LD6B	ECW	H33/25RD	Jun-54	Nov-75	Nov-76
7	UOD 500	Bristol Lodekka LD6B	ECW	H33/27RD	Mar-57	Nov-76	Feb-80
8	273 AUF	Leyland Leopard PSU3/1R	Marshall	B49F	Mar-63	Mar-77	May-78
9	BUF 272C	Leyland Titan PD3/4	Northern Counties	FH39/30F	Apr-65	Jul-78	Jul-93
10	PCK 384	Leyland Titan PD3/5	Metro-Cammell	FH41/31F	Jun-61	Jan-80	Jan-86
11	GRY 55D	Leyland Titan PD3A/1	Metro-Cammell	H41/33RD	Jun-66	Jul-80	Jul-94
12	HCD 356E	Leyland Titan PD3/4	Northern Counties	FH39/30F	Jul-67	Jan-81	Aug-91
13	AHA 451J	Leyland Leopard PSU4B/4R	Plaxton Panorama Elite II	C40F	May-71	Aug-83	Jun-97
14	AHA 452J	Leyland Leopard PSU4B/4R	Plaxton Panorama Elite II	C40F	May-71	Dec-85	Aug-94
15	WLT 655	AEC Routemaster	Park Royal	H36/28R	Jan-61	Aug-85	**Current**
16	WTN 640H	Leyland Atlantean PDR2/1	Alexander	H48/30D	Dec-69	Dec-85	Dec-00
17	WLT 621	AEC Routemaster	Park Royal	H36/28R	Jan-61	May-86	Oct-90
18	VWM 83L	Leyland Atlantean AN68/1R	Alexander	H45/29D	May-73	Aug-88	Sep-01
19	VWM 89L	Leyland Atlantean AN68/1R	Alexander	H45/29D	May-73	Aug-88	May-01
20	OTO 540M	Leyland Atlantean AN68/1R	East Lancs	H47/30D	Dec-73	Mar-89	Feb-01
21	GVO 717N	Leyland Atlantean AN68/1R	East Lancs	H47/31D	Mar-75	Jan-90	Feb-02
22	OTO 570M	Leyland Atlantean AN68/1R	East Lancs	H47/30D	Mar-74	Jun-90	May-05
23	HOR 305N	Leyland Atlantean AN68/1R	Alexander	H45/30D	May-75	Apr-91	Mar-02
24	HOR 306N	Leyland Atlantean AN68/1R	Alexander	H45/30D	Jun-75	Apr-91	Oct-02
25	KSA 183P	Leyland Atlantean AN68/1R	Alexander	H45/29D	Jan-76	Aug-91	Apr-03
26	OTO 557M	Leyland Atlantean AN68/1R	East Lancs	H47/30D	Feb-74	Oct-92	Oct-02
27	OTO 551M	Leyland Atlantean AN68/1R	East Lancs	H47/30D	Jan-74	Oct-92	Jul-06
28	OTO 562M	Leyland Atlantean AN68/1R	East Lancs	H47/30D	Feb-74	Aug-93	Feb-03
29	MNU 625P	Leyland Atlantean AN68/1R	East Lancs	H47/31D	Feb-76	May-94	Oct-03
30	MNU 631P	Leyland Atlantean AN68/1R	East Lancs	H47/31D	Mar-76	May-94	May-02
31	XRR 616M	Leyland Leopard PSU3B/4R	Plaxton Elite Express III	C53F	Aug-73	Aug-94	Jan-02
32	UVO 125S	Leyland Leopard PSU3E/4R	Duple Dominant Express	C49F	Nov-77	Aug-94	Oct-98
33	MNU 632P	Leyland Atlantean AN68/1R	East Lancs	H47/31D	Feb-76	Sep-94	Feb-03
34	KAU 564V	Leyland Leopard PSU3E/4R	Plaxton Supreme IV Express	C53F	Jul-80	Mar-96	Apr-06
35	LNU 569W	Leyland Leopard PSU3E/4R	Plaxton Supreme IV Express	C53F	Sep-80	Mar-96	Jun-03
36	VRC 611Y	Leyland Leopard PSU3G/4R	Plaxton Supreme V Express	C53F	Sep-82	Nov-96	Nov-07
37	PTV 591X	Leyland Leopard PSU3F/4R	Plaxton Supreme IV Express	C53F	Sep-81	Sep-97	Mar-07
38	A511 VKG	Leyland Olympian ONLXB/1R	East Lancs	H43/31F	Jan-84	Sep-98	Jul-07
39	RBO 510Y	Leyland Olympian ONLXB/1R	East Lancs	H43/31F	Feb-83	Mar-99	Aug-08
40	BWT 199X	Volvo B10M-61	Van Hool T8 Alizee	C48FT	Sep-81	Mar-99	May-14
41	A118 PBW	Leyland Tiger TRCTL11/3RH	Plaxton Paramount 3500 Express	C51F	Jun-84	Jan-00	Oct-13
42	VJO 205X	Leyland Olympian ONLXB/1R	ECW	H47/31F	Jun-82	Mar-00	Feb-13
43	C248 CKH	Leyland Tiger TRCTL11/3RZ	Plaxton Paramount II 3500	C49FT	Aug-85	Sep-00	Jan-07
44	FUM 490Y	Leyland Olympian ONLXB/1R	ECW	H45/29F	Apr-83	Dec-00	Mar-08
45	B124 UUD	Leyland Tiger TRCTL11/3RH	Plaxton Paramount II 3200 Express	C53F	Dec-84	Apr-01	Sep-11
46	UWW 8X	Leyland Olympian ONLXB/1R	Roe	H47/29F	Mar-82	Apr-01	**Current**
47	UWW 10X	Leyland Olympian ONLXB/1R	Roe	H47/29F	Mar-82	Sep-01	Aug-18
48	AEF 224Y	Leyland Olympian ONLXB/1R	ECW	H45/32F	May-83	Sep-01	Apr-15

49	XWY 476X	Leyland Olympian ONLXB/1R	ECW	H45/32F	May-82	Sep-01	Sep-18
50	A112 MUD	Leyland Tiger TRCTL11/3RH	Plaxton Paramount 3200 Express	C57F	Jan-84	Jan-02	Sep-11
51	EEH 903Y	Leyland Olympian ONLXB/1R	ECW	H45/32F	Jul-83	Jan-02	Mar-11
52	EEH 904Y	Leyland Olympian ONLXB/1R	ECW	H45/32F	Jun-83	Feb-02	**Spares**
53	UWW 9X	Leyland Olympian ONLXB/1R	Roe	H47/29F	Mar-82	Apr-02	Nov-17
54	E157 OMD	Leyland Olympian ONLXB/1RH	Optare	H47/29F	Apr-88	May-02	Aug-18
55	C71 CHM	Leyland Olympian ONLXB/1RH	ECW	H42/30F	May-86	Jul-02	**Current**
56	B123 UUD	Leyland Tiger TRCTL11/3RH	Plaxton Paramount II 3200 Express	C57F	Dec-84	Aug-02	Oct-10
57	A139 SMA	Leyland Olympian ONLXB/1R	ECW	H45/32F	Nov-83	Nov-02	**Spares**
58	JFR 5W	Leyland Olympian ONLXB/1R	ECW	H45/32F	Jul-81	Feb-03	Mar-09
59	DCZ 2319	Leyland Tiger TRCTL11/2RH	Plaxton Paramount 3200 Express	C53F	Jan-84	Apr-03	Oct-11
60	DCZ 2317	Leyland Tiger TRCTL11/2RH	Plaxton Paramount 3200 Express	C53F	Jan-84	Apr-03	Dec-16
61	CUD 221Y	Leyland Olympian ONLXB/1R	ECW	H47/31F	Jan-83	Oct-03	**Current**
62	MJI 7846	Leyland Tiger TRCTL11/3RH	Duple Laser	C53F	Aug-85	May-04	Jan-15
63	A502 EJF	Leyland Olympian ONLXB/1R	ECW	H45/32F	Oct-83	Sep-04	Dec-14
64	K561 GSA	Volvo B10M-60	Plaxton Premier Interurban	C51F	Feb-93	Jun-05	Sep-16
65	A132 SMA	Leyland Olympian ONLXB/1R	ECW	H45/32F	Sep-83	Aug-05	Oct-10
66	K562 GSA	Volvo B10M-60	Plaxton Premier Interurban	C51F	Feb-93	Feb-06	Sep-17
67	BBW 216Y	Leyland Olympian ONLXB/1R	ECW	H47/31F	Oct-82	Jul-06	Dec-16
68	L151 HUD	Volvo B10M-62	Plaxton Premier 350	C55F	Dec-93	Feb-07	Aug-19
69	B187 BLG	Leyland Olympian ONLXB/1R	ECW	H45/32F	Dec-84	Mar-08	**Current**
70	B190 BLG	Leyland Olympian ONLXB/1R	ECW	H45/32F	Jan-85	Mar-08	**Current**
71	FJ58 CON	Volvo B9TL	Optare Olympus	DPH47/30F	Dec-08	Dec-08	Jul-18
72	V125 MEV	Dennis Trident 2	Alexander ALX400	H47/31F	Nov-99	Dec-09	**Current**
73	L154 HUD	Volvo B10M-62	Plaxton Premier 350	C55F	Dec-93	Nov-11	**Current**
74	F127 PHM	Volvo Citybus B10M-50	Alexander RV	H46/40F	Oct-88	Oct-12	Oct-19
75	V110 LGC	Volvo B7TL	Alexander ALX400	H43/27F	Jan-00	Nov-12	**Current**
76	D137 FYM	Leyland Olympian ONLXB/1RH	ECW	H42/29F	Sep-86	Nov-12	**Current**
77	V188 OOE	Volvo B7TL	Alexander ALX400	H43/27F	Feb-00	May-14	**Current**
78	V208 OOE	Volvo B7TL	Alexander ALX400	H43/27F	Mar-00	Mar-14	**Current**
79	T308 YAW	Volvo Olympian OLY-50	Alexander Belfast RH	H47/34F	Aug-99	Apr-15	**Current**
80	L671 OHL	Volvo B10M-62	Plaxton Premier 320	C70F	Apr-94	Apr-16	**Current**
81	T479 KDM	Volvo Olympian OLY-50	Alexander Belfast RH	H47/27D	Mar-99	Aug-16	**Current**
82	V311 JMB	Volvo Olympian OLY-50	Alexander Belfast RH	H47/31F	Dec-99	Aug-16	**Current**
83	V363 JMB	Volvo Olympian OLY-50	Alexander Belfast RH	H47/27D	Dec-99	Aug-16	**Current**
84	V364 JMB	Volvo Olympian OLY-50	Alexander Belfast RH	H47/27D	Dec-99	Aug-16	**Current**
85	S213 JUA	DAF DE02RSDB250	Alexander ALX400	H45/23F	Nov-98	Nov-16	**Current**
86	S214 JUA	DAF DE02RSDB250	Alexander ALX400	H45/21F	Nov-98	Nov-16	**Current**
87	V132 LGC	Volvo B7TL	Alexander ALX400	H47/27F	Jan-00	Nov-17	**Current**
88	V144 LGC	Volvo B7TL	Alexander ALX400	H47/27F	Feb-00	Nov-17	**Current**
89	T325 LAF	Volvo B10M-62	Berkhof Axial 50	C53F	May-99	Oct-18	**Current**
90	T478 KDM	Volvo Olympian OLY-50	Alexander Belfast RH	H47/31F	Mar-99	Apr-19	**Current**

Other buses acquired for spares (S) or on loan (L)

L	GVO 719N	Leyland Atlantean AN68/1R	East Lancs	H47/31D	Mar-75	Mar-90	Jun-90
S	UVO 128S	Leyland Leopard PSU3E/4R	Duple Dominant Express	C49F	Nov-77	Aug-94	Sep-94
L	KYN 288X	Leyland Titan TNLXB2RR	Leyland	H44/24F	Aug-81	Jan-01	Jun-01
L	CUL 143V	Leyland Titan TNLXB2RRsp	Park Royal	H44/26F	Jan-80	Jun-01	Sep-01
S	D80 UTF	Leyland Olympian ONLXCT/1RH	ECW	CH39/27F	Aug-86	Dec-02	Jan-03
S	JTY 371X	Leyland Olympian ONLXB/1R	ECW	H45/32F	Jan-82	Oct-07	Aug-10
S	W132 EON	Volvo B7TL	Alexander ALX400	H43/20D	Mar-00	Jul-15	**Spares**

Fleet Statistics

A few graphs help to demonstrate how the fleet has evolved between May 1970 and January 2020. The first graph depicts the top ten longest serving buses. The Operational fleet size by month confirms the highest number of buses owned was 35 in March 2006. The timeline shows the size of the fleet each year, including June 2003 when the firm was incorporated.

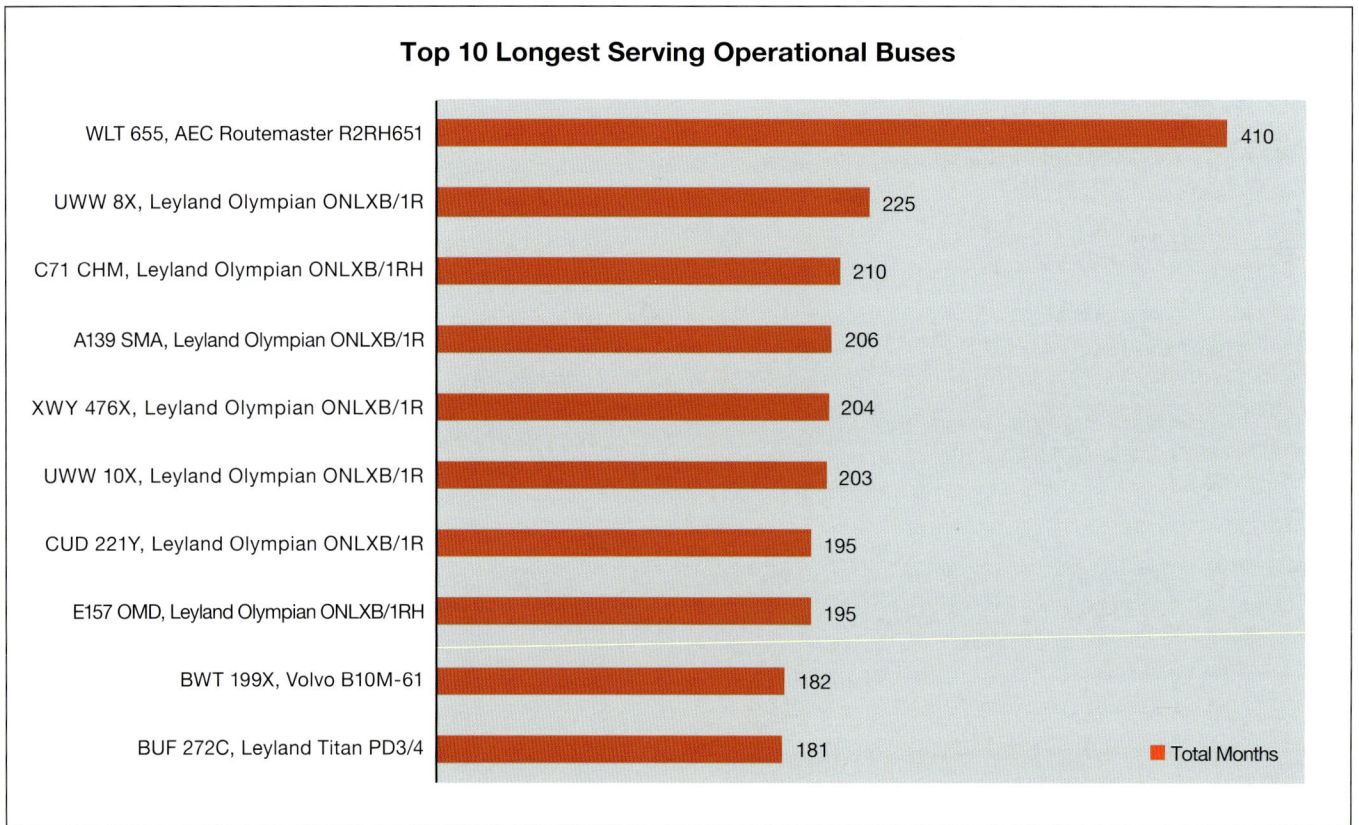

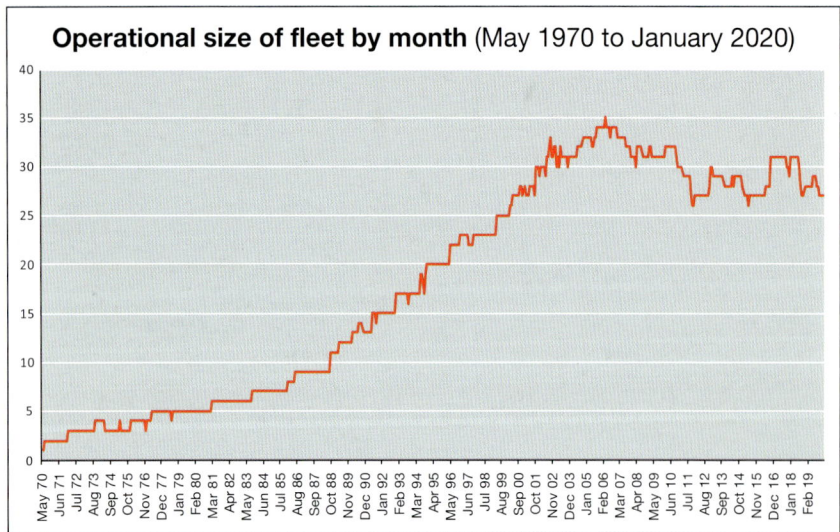

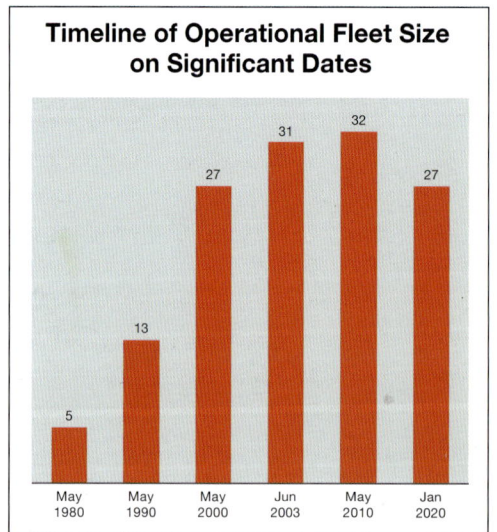

Top 10 Longest Serving Operational Buses

Bus	Total Months
WLT 655, AEC Routemaster R2RH651	410
UWW 8X, Leyland Olympian ONLXB/1R	225
C71 CHM, Leyland Olympian ONLXB/1RH	210
A139 SMA, Leyland Olympian ONLXB/1R	206
XWY 476X, Leyland Olympian ONLXB/1R	204
UWW 10X, Leyland Olympian ONLXB/1R	203
CUD 221Y, Leyland Olympian ONLXB/1R	195
E157 OMD, Leyland Olympian ONLXB/1RH	195
BWT 199X, Volvo B10M-61	182
BUF 272C, Leyland Titan PD3/4	181

Operational size of fleet by month (May 1970 to January 2020)

Timeline of Operational Fleet Size on Significant Dates

Date	Fleet Size
May 1980	5
May 1990	13
May 2000	27
Jun 2003	31
May 2010	32
Jan 2020	27

Preserved Buses and Coaches

With vehicles being operated and well maintained for many years it is not surprising that 26 have, at some stage, been acquired for preservation, representing a staggering 29% of the total fleet.

Unfortunately, 12 of these vehicles have not survived, although at least five still exist, but the remaining 14 are still around for you to enjoy.

PUF 647	Guy Arab IV/Park Royal	Southdown
749 DCD	Leyland Leopard/Harrington	Southdown
273 AUF	Leyland Leopard/Marshall	Southdown
BUF 272C	Leyland Titan PD3/Northern Counties	Southdown
HCD 356E	Leyland Titan PD3/Northern Counties	Southdown
AHA 451J	Leyland Leopard/Plaxton Panorama Elite	Midland Red
VWM 83L	Leyland Atlantean/Alexander	Southport
OTO 540M	Leyland Atlantean/East Lancs.	Nottingham
KAU 564V	Leyland Leopard/Plaxton Supreme	Barton
UWW 10X	Leyland Olympian/Roe	West Yorkshire PTE
XWY 476X	Leyland Olympian/ECW	West Riding
A502 EJF	Leyland Olympian/ECW	Midland Fox
DCZ 2317		
(ex A127 EPA)	Leyland Tiger/Plaxton Paramount	London Country
E157 OMD	Leyland Olympian/Optare	Maidstone

The vehicles that sadly have not survived in preservation are:

WLT 621	AEC Routemaster/Park Royal	London Transport
GRY 55D	Leyland Titan PD3/Metro-Cammell	Leicester
VWM 89L	Leyland Atlantean/Alexander	Southport
OTO 557M	Leyland Atlantean/East Lancs.	Nottingham
OTO 570M	Leyland Atlantean/East Lancs.	Nottingham
HOR 305N	Leyland Atlantean/Alexander	Portsmouth
HOR 306N	Leyland Atlantean/Alexander	Portsmouth
MNU 625P	Leyland Atlantean/East Lancs.	Nottingham
PTV 591X	Leyland Leopard/Plaxton Supreme	Barton
VRC 611Y	Leyland Leopard/Plaxton Supreme	Barton
RBO 510Y	Leyland Olympian/East Lancs.	Cardiff
DCZ 2319		
(ex A126 EPA)	Leyland Tiger/Plaxton Paramount	London Country

We have included photographs of many of the restored vehicles in the appropriate sections of the detailed fleet history. This photograph shows Ken Williams with four Southdown vehicles that he operated at the Southdown Centenary Rally on Southsea Common on 7 June 2015. From left to right they were No 5 (749 DCD), No 1 (PUF 647), No 9 (BUF 272C) and No 12 (HCD 356E). Simon Gill

Confidence Driving Record – 3 Weeks in 1996

Former driver, Richard Worman, has kindly given us access to his driving record during three weeks of 1996 when he drove for Confidence. It gives us an insight as to what vehicles and services a driver can provide. Were you one of his passengers?

DATE	FLEET NO	ROUTES MORNING	ROUTES AFTERNOON	NOTES
4 March	20 (OTO 540M)	Empty to Wigston - Post House. Then as passenger S60 to Judgemeadow. Three swims Thurnby Lodge to Evington baths and return	Swim Sparkenhoe St. to Spence St. and return. Then S68 St.Josephs to Coleman Rd. Then as passenger S68 Judgemeadow to Victoria Park	
5 March	24 (HOR 306N)	S224 South Wigston - St.Pauls Moat - St.Margarets Baths Spinney Hill - Jewry Wall St.Margarets Baths - Moat Empty to Spalding St.	Humberstone Jnr - Spence St. x2 Spence St - Humberstone Jnr x2 S224 15.30 St.Pauls - South Wigston	
6 March	30 (MNU 631P)	Empty to Wigston - Houghton. S292 Houghton - Gartree Empty to Wigston.		
	20 (OTO 540M)		Charnwood School - St.Margarets S224 15.30 St.Pauls - South Wigston	
7 March	29 (MNU 625P)	S225 Blaby - St.Pauls		Empty to Wigston.
	15 (WLT 655)		13.15 Ravenhurst - Winstanley 13.30 Ravenhurst - Winstanley 13.50 Ravenhurst - Winstanley 14.15 Winstanley - Ravenhurst 14.30 Ravenhurst - Winstanley 14.45 Winstanley - Ravenhurst 15.00 Winstanley - Ravenhurst 15.15 Winstanley - Ravenhurst	
8 March	15 (WLT 655)	Empty to Wigston - Houghton. S292 Houghton - Gartree	Stoneygate College - Manor Rd Play Field Manor Rd Play Field - Stoneygate College S292 Gartree - Houghton.	
17 June	35 (LNU 569W)	08.15 Stoneygate Sch - Great Glen 09.30 Langmoor - Abbey Park 10.30 St.Thomas Moore - Misterton Hall	15.30 Misterton Hall - St.Thomas Moore	Empty Wigston to Stoneygate school, then empty Great Glen to Langmoor. Empty to St.Thomas Moore. Empty back to Wigston
18 June	31 (XRR 616M)	09.00 Uplands Jnr - Beaumanor Hall	14.30 Beaumanor Hall - Uplands Jnr	
19 June	27 (OTO 551M)	S223 Welford Rd - St.Pauls S68 Coleman Rd - St.Josephs 09.25 St.John Baptist - Stonehurst Farm	14.30 Stonehurst Farm - St.John Baptist C1 15.30 Oadby Schools - Green Lane Rd	
20 June	34 (KAU 564V)	08.30 Sacred Heart - Ashbourne	15.00 Ashbourne - Sacred Heart	
21 June	29 (MNU 625P)	08.15 Stoneygate Sch - Great Glen 09.25 Launde School - Haymarket	12.00 Aylestone Baths - St.Crispins 12.35 Uppingham Rd - Gilroes 14.35 Gilroes - Uppingham Rd S225 15.30 St.Pauls - Blaby	Funeral Funeral
24 June	27 (OTO 551M)	S224 South Wigston - St.Pauls. 09.10 Spinney hill - Twycross Zoo	14.00 Twycross Zoo - Spinney Hill S224 15.30 St.Pauls - South Wigston	
25 June	29 (MNU 625P)	S224 South Wig - St.Pauls. 08.50 Moat - Welford Rd Fields 10.15 Welford Rd Fields - Moat 10.50 Moat - Welford Rd Fields 11.30 Eng.Martyrs - Saffron Lane Sta.	12.15 Welford Rd Fields - Moat 14.45 Saffron Lane Sta. - Eng.Martyrs. 15.05 Saffron Lane Sta. - Eng.Martyrs.	
26 June	29 (MNU 625P)	S224 South Wigston - St.Pauls 10.15 Old Mill Sch. - Hinckley Leics. 11.45 Hinckley Leics. - Old Mill Sch	13.45 Stoneygate Sch. - Great Glen 15.05 Great Glen - Stoneygate Sch	
27 June	34 (KAU 564V)	S224 South Wigston - St.Pauls. Empty to Spalding St.	13.30 Narborough Rd - Saffron Hill Cem. 15.00 Saffron Hill Cem. - Sawday St. S225 15.30 St.Pauls - Blaby.	Funeral Funeral, then empty to St Pauls to replace booked vehicle. Dep.St.Pauls 15.55 Broke down.
28 June	31 (XRR 616M)	S224 South Wigston - St.Pauls.	Assist on S52,S223 and S290. As passenger	End of term.